18350916

THE PRACTICAL
STRATEGIST

THE PRACTICAL STRATEGIST

Business and Corporate Strategy for the 1990s

ROBERT J. ALLIO

1817

Harper & Row, Publishers, New York

BALLINGER DIVISION

Grand Rapids, Philadelphia, St. Louis, San Francisco
London, Singapore, Sydney, Tokyo, Toronto

International Standard Book Number: 0–88730–319–6 (cloth)
0–88730–399–4 (paper)

Library of Congress Catalog Card Number: 88–24200

Printed in the United States of America

Library of Congress Cataloging-in-Publication Data

Allio, Robert J.

The practical strategist.

Includes index.
ISBN 0–88730–319–6 (cloth)
ISBN 0–88730–399–4 (paper)
1. Strategic planning.   I. Title.

HG30.28.A384   658.4'012   88–24200

89 90 91 92 HC 9 8 7 6 5 4 3 2 1

To Barbara

CONTENTS

LIST OF FIGURES

LIST OF TABLES

PREFACE

This primer on practical strategy summarizes the results of twenty years of work with organizations that have sought economic and managerial renewal. Part I presents the theory and practice of business strategy, while Part II addresses the less familiar arena of corporate strategy. In Part III, I conclude with the essential elements of how strategy must be implemented to achieve superior performance.

My purpose in this book is to satisfy the formal definition of practical: *capable of being used or put into effect*. Yet at the same time, I have striven to identify the fundamental concepts that underlie the selection of effective strategy. Thus, the governing criteria for including material in this book are twofold:

1) Is it practical?
2) Does it make sense?

Who should read this treatise? The manager of any organization, be it a small single-business firm or a large multinational corporation, will find practical strategies (not an oxymoron!) that lead to better results. And the student will find organizing principles to demonstrate that the art of strategy formulation has become a virtual science.

In physics, one discovery leads us deeper and deeper in our search for a unified field theory and the true nature of matter. Similarly, in the domain of strategy, although I contend that rigorous theories of economic and social behavior can be identified, one insight leads to another and still another. This phenomenon was expressed once by Zeno in his parable of Achilles, who was never able to overtake the tortoise since it always moved a small distance further whenever Achilles was about to catch up with him. Thus, the field of strategy continues to develop, as illustrated by the recent use of game theory to understand the tradeoffs between competition and collaboration and the application of artificial intelligence to create expert systems for making business decisions. This book represents the best current technology—but I urge colleagues, students, and managers to be alert to new developments.

My clients have contributed materially to this project by challenging me to innovate and extend some of my original prescriptions, refusing to be constrained by procrustean formulas. Discussions with Tom Bell at Dominion Textile, Jairo Estrada at Garden Way, George Hegg at 3M, and Diego Suárez at V. Suárez & Co. have been particularly helpful. A number of my colleagues, including Paul Allio, David Amar, Allan Cohen, Jeffery Ellis, Karen Goncalves, Daniel Muzyka, Robert Reiser, George Sawyer, Joel Shulman, and Natalie Taylor have skillfully reviewed many sections of this book. And I am also grateful to the undergraduate and graduate students at Babson College; they have endured earlier versions of my concepts and have justly demanded greater clarity.

Finally, I want to acknowledge the singular contributions of my assistant, Diane Grant, in managing the project, the success of Nicholas Gargour in producing the fine graphics, and the valuable editorial counsel of Marjorie Richman at Ballinger Publishing Company.

THE PRACTICAL
STRATEGIST

1 THE CHALLENGE OF MANAGING IN THE 1990s

As a manager looking forward into the 1990s, it is easy to feel intimidated by the dramatic and imposing challenges that are likely to be encountered. For the history of managerial response to new situations has been a disappointment. When faced with change, few managers respond as architects and builders for the future—most well-known role models become caretakers instead. They attach themselves mindlessly to old strategies and modes of behavior, and they react passively to new challenges and opportunities. Those of us who are willing to take the risk of managing creatively are pioneers, with few obvious lessons from the past to guide us.

This book describes in pragmatic terms what achieving superior performance really means. It is designed for the practical strategist, the manager who recognizes that finding effective strategies for today's situation is not enough. He or she must also exhibit the will, resolution, skill, and leadership to implement them as well. In addition, the practical strategist must be prepared to adapt to change and to respond creatively to unexpected and unforeseen events.

EMERGING ISSUES AND CHALLENGES

The scenario for the next decade will be marked by slow growth in Western markets, offset by rapid growth in markets of the Pacific. This

1

is already triggering a transformation to global competition and global strategy. Many inefficient enterprises will be forced out of market; most of the 15 million U.S. businesses do not perform well, even in today's relatively tolerant environment. Others, attempting to survive, will be swept up in the rising tide of consolidation and merger. And economic control will shift from U.S. capitalists to non-U.S. capitalists who are benefiting from the reduced value of the U.S. dollar. The Japanese, British, Canadians, and Australians have been in the vanguard of this trend.

Some Critical Issues

Declining Markets.   The phenomenon of the declining market is already palpable to the managers in textiles, steel, electric utilities, and a multitude of other industries. The inevitable reduction in corporate growth in such industries has lowered market values and engendered a host of takeovers and restructurings. Existing competitors must work harder to maintain their share of these slower growing markets, while shorter product life cycles place a premium on agility.

Deregulation.   The free market in the United States has already precipitated a new way of life for airlines, banking, telecommunications, trucking, health care, and other industries that, for the first time in their corporate lives, are being exposed to a rising tide of competition. The shift toward open competition is mirrored around the world, and even the USSR is encouraging decentralization of authority from central planners to local factory managers who can negotiate suppliers' prices, set production levels, and begin to compete in free markets.

Globalization.   U.S. managers in farm equipment, automobiles, consumer electronics, and other industries are experiencing a homogenization of markets around the world and a standardization of products. As a result, foreign competitors have appeared on the scene to exacerbate the already intense competition that accompanies market maturity. Yet, at the same time, increasing market diversity is demanding greater flexibility and responsiveness to customers.

Dwindling Resources.   In the long term, corporations may suffer from a scarcity of critical raw materials. But in the short term, skilled human resources—and competent managers, in particular—may constitute the most critical shortage.

Environmental Distress.   Asbestos, acid rain, carcinogens, nuclear fall-out, all have combined to arouse a once passive public. Law suits are multiplying in an already litigious society, and in many industries, such as health care, the cost of liability insurance is reaching intolerable levels.

Capital Surfeit.   The successful players in mature industries now face the need to constructively dispose of a mounting abundance of cash, a situation that presents interesting opportunities for these firms. A growing trend toward diversification by acquisition, despite the limited success of this strategy, has been one of the responses.

THE STRATEGIC RESPONSE

Under these conditions, selecting good *strategy (S)* is a prerequisite to superior *performance (P)*. But achieving high performance is not a matter of good strategy alone. It demands good *implementation (I)* as well.

$$P = S \times I.$$

Unfortunately, firms are often stymied in achieving better perform-ance by an apparent dichotomy in roles within the organization. The heads of corporations and businesses are occupied with developing strategy (or they should be!). On the other hand, line managers at every level are charged with implementation—carrying out business and cor-porate strategy. Good strategy emerges when corporate, business, and line managers step back and look at the broad picture. Yet implementa-tion requires that managers focus on details. Above all, good perform-ance requires linking strategy and implementation.

Thus, improving performance in the 1990s will require that managers think strategically, in itself a new challenge for many. Indeed, a recent Conference Board survey of top management identified the need for a strategic business planning perspective as today's greatest challenge for top management.[1] But managers must also do a better job of imple-menting strategy. The *practical strategist* finds effective strategies and is adept at implementation as well. Such a manager not only *thinks* strategically, in other words, but *behaves* strategically as well.

It is hard to find exemplars of this necessary competence in both for-mulating strategy and attending to the details of implementation, par-ticularly throughout the entire period of an organization's evolution.

Apple under Steve Jobs conceived a brilliant strategy. But only when John Scully arrived to give attention to implementation did Jobs' strategies begin to produce good results. Anheuser-Busch performed adequately until the Miller challenge of the 1970s. But under Augie Busch, the firm sharpened its strategy, maintained efficiency, and drove to a position of leadership. Lew Lehr at 3M led the corporation into a number of related new growth sectors, including health care; but only under Allen Jacobson has balanced attention been given to implementation. The short list of executives who do appear to balance strategy formulation and implementation includes James Burke of Johnson and Johnson, Lee Iacocca of Chrysler, Ken Olsen of Digital Equipment Corporation, (despite some uneven results in the early 1980s), and Jack Welch of General Electric. Bill Gates at Microsoft may be another candidate, although definitive assessment of his performance is perhaps premature.

THE HIERARCHY OF STRATEGIC ACTIVITY

In any organization we can identify a system of managerial activities and priorities (Figure 1–1). At the corporate level, executives are concerned with managing the resources of the firm, making decisions about what economic games to play and how much to invest in each game. This constitutes the domain of corporate strategy. But corporations do not compete in the marketplace for customers (although they may compete for human resources or financial resources); rather, it is businesses of various corporations that compete against one another. Thus General Electric, from the corporate strategy perspective, no longer competes directly with Westinghouse Electric, although their power generation equipment divisions (their businesses) do compete. GE makes light bulbs, while Westinghouse does not. Conversely, Westinghouse bottles soft drinks but GE does not.

It is useful, therefore, to view the corporation as comprising a set of businesses. *Corporate strategy* is concerned primarily with the selection of economic activities (businesses) that best satisfy the needs of the corporation's stakeholders (its stockholders and employees, as well as customers, suppliers, and the community) and the allocation of resources to maximize stakeholders' value. *Business strategy*, on the other hand, is concerned with how to create and deliver products and services to external customers in the face of competition. Even in a single-business corporation, the distinction between business strategy and corporate strategy is useful.

Figure 1–1. The Corporate Strategy Components.

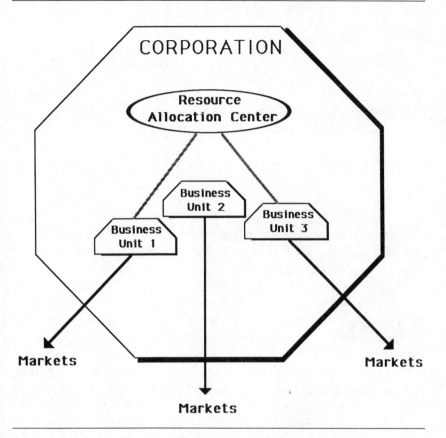

THE LOGIC OF STRATEGY DEVELOPMENT

If the strategic development process were linear, the sequence of activities would be represented by Figure 1–2. In reality, however, some strategies are already in place—an organization almost never starts with a blank slate, *ex nihilo,* except in the possible case of a new venture. Nevertheless, we should begin ideally with the task of formulating business strategy, for it is at this level that the corporation is exposed to direct competition in the market. Most of the corporation's assets (financial and managerial) are committed to its businesses, and it is the businesses that generate or consume cash.

Figure 1–2. The Corporate Planning Process.

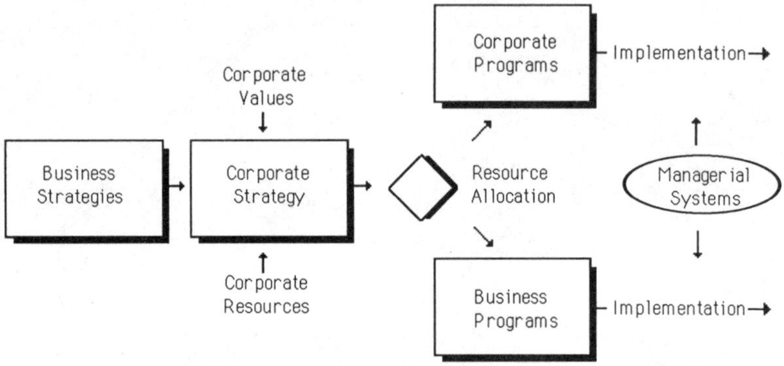

The input from business-level managers is then modified if necessary, ratified, supported, and coordinated at the corporate level. Business managers are thus given the opportunity to formulate an optimal strategy in the absence of preconceived arbitrary goals or resource constraints. It is inappropriate for the corporation to set goals or select strategies for the business in advance of recommendations from the business managers, although the corporation can identify its aspirations and the level of risk that it is willing to tolerate. Inherent in our model is the precept that strategy selection be neither mandated by corporate management (top-down) nor assembled from the inputs of functional managers (bottom-up).

The strategies proposed by each of the corporation's businesses constitute input to corporate strategy. During formulation of corporate strategy, planners evaluate the alternative uses of corporate resources in the light of both the corporate value system (What is important?) and the discretionary resources available (How much can we afford to invest?). Business managers in effect compete for the use of corporate resources by the quality of their strategies.

Once resources are allocated to business strategies that are consistent with corporate strategy or to other corporate programs, the implementation process can begin. Implementation will take the form of action programs supported by appropriate managerial systems. In a well-managed corporation, all the activities of the firm are linked to strategy; that is, they support either corporate or business strategies. Conversely, all strategies of the firm are supported by specific programs or sets of activities.[2]

PATTERNS AND CONNECTIONS

A practical strategist needs to acquire two skills that are powerful adjuncts to developing and implementing of effective strategy. These are the ability to *discern patterns* and the ability to *see connections.*

The best quiltmakers create marvelous patterns from a random collection of scraps of cloth and other artifacts. Similarly, an essential skill for coping with the morass of data that confronts the manager in today's information age is pattern recognition. Perceiving or creating order and value places heavy demands on deductive ability as opposed to inductive ability. The logical process of pattern recognition is one aspect of strategic reasoning.

The corollary to the need for pattern recognition is that we apprehend the *system* we are attempting to manage and examine the linkages or connections (that is, avoid looking only at the pieces). The important linkages can be grouped into four categories.

1. *Vertical* linkages—between corporate or business strategy and the operating programs or activities that implement strategy.
2. *External* linkages—between the organization as a whole and the external forces that bear on it. The ability of the organization to resonate with its environment determines how well it will survive and flourish.
3. *Lateral* connections—among the several elements of the organization, for example, among the different businesses of the firm or its various functions. Sharing leads to synergy.
4. *Temporal* connections—between the organization as it is today, was yesterday, and may be in the future. Every organization must pay homage to its past and accept itself as an evolving organism along the continuum of time.

Apprehending the organization as a part of a total system, all the parts of which are connected, will yield rich insights for a practical strategist.

A primary purpose of the book is to guide managers to appreciate the patterns and connections that lead to practical strategies for their businesses and corporations. Included is a portfolio of technologies and examples of practical strategy. A glossary of frequently used terms is presented in Table 1–1.

Table 1–1. The Language of Strategy.

Industry—a set of business competitors. They may participate in the same or in different market segments with the same or different products or services.

Market—the customers served by the industry. Segments often can be distinguished by geography, distribution channels, customer characteristics, or product type.

Competitor—a business that offers to satisfy customers' needs with an alternative product or service, offering the customer a choice.

Business—the activities required to sell a set of related products or services to similar markets against common competitors.

Strategy—a set of decisions and behavior (what managers and organizations do); a pattern of resource allocation.

NOTES

1. Harold Stieglitz, *"Chief Executives View Their Jobs: Today and Tomorrow,"* (Research Report, The Conference Board, 1985), p. 14.
2. From a systems point of view, this is merely an expression of Ashby's Law of Requisite Variety. See W. Ross Ashby, *An Introduction to Cybernetics,* (London: Chapman and Hall, 1956), p. 53.

1 BUSINESS STRATEGY

Developing strategy for a business follows a simple four-step logic.

1. *Business unit description.* What is the scope of the business? How is the industry best defined, and in what segments of the industry is the business positioned? (What's the game and where have we chosen to play?)
2. *Situation analysis.* What are the important characteristics of the industry, the markets and the competition? What distinctive competencies does the business offer? (Remember that a resource audit, an assessment of strengths and weaknesses, is only meaningful relative to competitors.) What future assumptions are reasonable; that is, what are the dynamics of the market and the competition? (How is the game played?)
3. *Strategy formulation.* What strategy makes the most sense from among all the reasonable alternatives? Can the firm achieve a sustainable advantage over competitors in the markets it has chosen to serve? (How can we win?)
4. *Investment and performance analysis.* What resources will be required to implement the strategy, and what results can be expected? Do the rewards justify the risk? (Can we afford to play?)

We will examine each of these elements in turn, keeping in mind that developing a strategy invariably demands trial and error as managers search for the best way to allocate resources and optimize performance.

2 BUSINESS SCOPE AND INDUSTRY DEFINITION

A successful corporation allocates resources to businesses, rather than to products, functions, organizational units, or capital projects. To do so effectively the corporation must first have segmented its products and services correctly into businesses and identified accurately the industries in which they compete, two critical steps in developing strategy.[1]

Clear specification of the industry sets the stage for selecting a strategy. Indeed, this decision plays a powerful and insidious role in biasing the strategy selection, for by its very nature the definition of the industry implies a definition of both the customers and the competitors. The business, of course, may opt to compete in product, market, or technology segments different from those selected by competitors. And if the segments are large enough to be attractive, performance will be improved by maximizing this difference.

Thus, after the corporation has selected the industry in which it wants to participate, its business managers must still select the scope of the business: how and where they choose to compete. Corporations in other words decide in which industries to participate, while the business managers decide how to participate.

DEFINING THE SCOPE OF A BUSINESS

In the typical corporation, individual products, product lines, or organizational units receive resources directly from the corporation. Although this policy optimizes the performance of a product in a particular market, it reduces business unit performance to less than its potential. Internal competition (between product managers, market managers, or functional managers) is fostered, when in fact victory over external competitors is more rewarding for the corporation. Often, opportunities for collaboration within the corporation are overlooked or ignored, necessitating allocation of additional corporate resources to manage linkages. As a consequence, the corporation as a whole does not perform as well as it might.

The remedy for this condition is to restructure the firm for the purposes of strategy development into businesses. In corporate jargon, businesses are sometimes labeled strategic business units (SBUs), strategy centers (SCs), or strategic business centers (SBCs). Regardless of the label, the task of proper business definition poses a challenge for corporations attempting to progress beyond the classic divisional approach to strategy, because it forces a thorough analysis of questions such as "Which products and services should be assigned to the business unit?" and "In what industry does the business compete?" Even the concept of a business may prove controversial. The following definition is a start:

A business is a set of related products and services marketed to similar customers against common competitors.

But a business must also meet other criteria. First, it must derive the majority of its revenue from sales outside the corporation. It must also have reasonable strategic autonomy (not be constrained by other businesses in the corporation), and it must control most of the resources needed to implement its strategies.

Hence any operation within the corporation that provides services or products only to other businesses within the corporation (centralized manufacturing plants and research and development laboratories) fails this test. This does not obviate the need for these organizations to prepare strategic plans. But the strategies for these resource centers or corporate functions cannot be developed autonomously—they depend upon and are determined by the strategies of the business units they serve.

Describing the business is relatively easy for the one-product firm. (For example, "We make and sell premium beer in Boston.") But suppose the firm has several products or services. Should they be grouped in one business unit or should each be viewed as a separate business? The logic for assigning products and services to a particular business unit involves tests of independence. As the linkage among products increases, they begin to fit more naturally under the umbrella of a single business. The following six guidelines can be applied:

1. *Customers.* Are products sold to similar customer groups?
2. *Competitors.* Are products sold to these customers against common competitors?
3. *Product function.* Do products perform the same function; that is, can they be substituted for one another? (Examples are gas ranges and electric ranges or passenger cars and light trucks.)
4. *Product characteristics.* Do products have similar selling features such as quality, style, and color? (Examples are washing machines and dryers.)
5. *Shared experience base.* Do products share manufacturing facilities, technology, distribution channels, promotion, or advertising? (Examples are the components for many General Motors cars.)

If all these linkages are strong, they suggest that products be combined into a single business unit in order to capitalize on the benefits of a coordinated approach to the market or to suppliers. If the evidence from these tests is still ambiguous or contradictory, we can invoke one final test:

6. *Strategic autonomy.* Can two products or services be managed independently, or do they interact strongly in the marketplace? Does a change in the price of one product alter the demand for another product? (Changing the price of the Ford affects demand for the Mercury, for example.) Similarly, changing the price for repair service or replacement parts changes the demand for the product itself.

The ultimate criterion is whether or not it makes sense for managers to develop a single strategy for a particular set of products and services—or alternatively, whether better performance can be expected if independent strategies are pursued for the individual products.

The approach taken by 3M's Life Sciences Sector to reconfigure its activities strategically is illustrated in Figure 2–1. A review of the products

Figure 2–1. Business Definition at 3M.

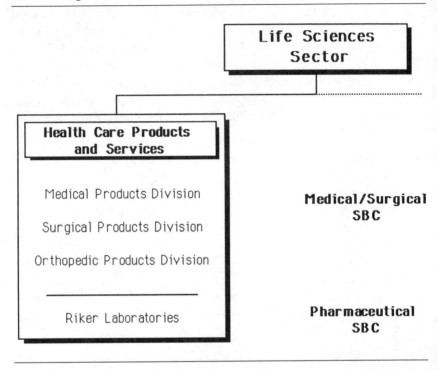

and markets served by the Medical Products, Surgical Products, Orthopedic Products, and Riker Laboratories units revealed that they faced many of the same competitors for the same customers. As a result, management established two business units (designated as strategic business centers, or SBCs) to coordinate the Life Science Sector's competitive strengths and opportunities. One SBC encompasses the sale of medical and surgical supplies to hospitals and doctors' offices. The second SBC sells pharmaceutical products to pharmacists and physicians.

GE made a similar move in 1972 when its three profit centers, for laundry products, refrigerators, and kitchen ranges, were combined into one home appliance business (designated as a strategic business unit, or SBU). The objective was to position GE more effectively against competitors who were approaching the market with broad product lines, unified distribution systems, and coordinated advertising and promotion.

Clearly, a business unit need not be synonymous with any of the elements displayed on the firm's organization chart. A business may be part of an organizational unit or it may embrace several organizations. Organization units are often designed to facilitate internal administration (break the span of control, for example) or satisfy political objectives, as opposed to optimizing external effectiveness. As a result, the organization need not be changed to conform to the business unit, provided all the activities within the organization are driven by a single strategy. Ultimately, though, organizations function more effectively when they coordinate strategy and structure. In other words, in the long run corporate performance improves when organizational elements and business units are the same.

An organizational unit that serves only the needs of other businesses within the corporation, having no external customers, is not itself a business. But what happens when this resource center (research and development, manufacturing, data processing) begins to market products or services outside the corporation? The initial external activity is justified because excess capacity or manpower is utilized and overhead is absorbed. As revenues from external sales become important, however, conflict arises if the primary role of the unit is not explicitly clear. Examining the rationale for the next increment of capital investment often helps to clarify corporate expectations; new investment approved on the basis of serving additional external customers gives a clear signal, for example.

IDENTIFYING THE INDUSTRY

Suppose we've succeeded in arriving at a reasonable description of the scope of the business. In what industry is the business competing? This apparently trivial query is often hard to answer. Suppose, to return to an earlier example, the firm makes and sells premium beer in Boston. Is it a competitor in the premium beer industry? The beer industry? Alcoholic beverages? Beverages? And does it make a difference how the firm's strategists define the industry?

It does indeed. In fact, proper identification of the industry is prerequisite to choosing effective strategies for a business. To be consistant with the original definition, we must specify

- Competitors
- Markets and suppliers
- Customer needs

Broadly defining an industry (packaging, office of the future, communications) risks dissipating energy on customers and competitors who do not materially affect a firm's performance. On the other hand, defining the industry narrowly (cans, copiers, telephones) risks ignoring dangerous competitors or important potential market segments.

The markets for an industry are usually specified in terms of geographic areas and customer types (male or female, upscale or downscale, industrial or consumer, for example). Customers needs are best expressed in terms of the benefits of the product or service (or the function it serves—for example, selling grass seed versus improving customers' lawns) and the technology required to satisfy this function.

Not all competitors in an industry serve exactly the same market segments, of course, and they are unlikely to adopt identical strategies. As a result, in a single industry we may observe substantial differences in competitors' breadth of product line, product quality, prices, and so forth. Apparent competitors, in fact, sometimes position themselves to sell as though they were in different industries, as witness the strategies of three watch producers: Timex (low price watches), Swatch (fashion accessories), and Patek Phillipe (jewelry). In the field of medical diagnostics, as another example, competitors serve physicians and hospitals (the markets) who seek to diagnose medical condition (the customer need) with a variety of technologies, both invasive (surgery, nuclear medicine) and noninvasive (x-ray, ultrasound, and magnetic resonance).

The concept of an arena was developed to describe a set of related industries, a segment of the economy. An arena display is helpful in identifying business units within the firm that may benefit from collaboration. It may also indicate possibilities for growth in related areas and sources of future competition. And the position of current competitors can be displayed. Figure 2–2 represents an arena map of information on the universe of competing products and technologies along both product/service and form/substance spectrums. Figure 2–3 depicts the arena of transportation, showing where General Motors had positioned itself in the early 1980s, before the acquisition of EDS and Hughes.

Identifying the industry is crucial if the industry is experiencing transformation because of exogenous factors such as regulation or deregulation. Consider the three industries represented in 1960 by AT&T (telephones), Xerox (office copiers), and IBM (data processing). By 1980

Figure 2–2. An Arena Map of Information.

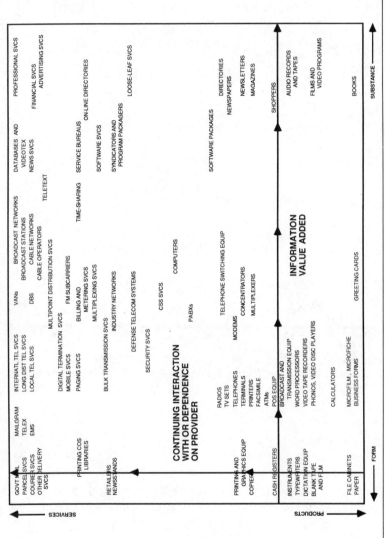

Figure 2–3.   An Arena Map of Transportation.

	Land	Sea	Air	Space
Services	Tourist and Travel Parking *Rental and Leasing Financial and Insurance Distribution and Retail*	Tourist and Travel Marinas *Rental and Leasing Financial and Insurance Distribution and Retail*	Tourist and Travel Airports *Rental and Leasing Financial and Insurance Distribution and Retail*	
Products	*Automobiles Buses Trucks Locomotives* Railroad Cars Motorcycles	Boats Ships Barges	Business Jets Aircraft Helicopters	Satellites Missiles Guns Rockets
Components	*Controls Drives Motors Diesels Structures*	*Diesels* Controls Guidance Steam Turbines Structures	*Jet Engines* Controls Guidance Motors Airframes	*Controls* Guidance Power –Supply –Structures
Parts	*Electrical* Tires Fuels	Electrical Fuels	Electrical Tires Fuels	Electrical Fuels

Italics : General Motors Corporation

Source: William E. Rothschild, *How to Gain (and Maintain) Competitive Advantage in Business* (New York: McGraw-Hill, 1984).

deregulation, advances in technology, and the behavior of major competitors produced a rapid convergence of these discrete industries into a single industry, information systems. Recent investments by IBM in Rolm and MCI are consistent with this shift of industry boundaries. Numerous examples of boundary shifts also can be found in the service industries, as illustrated by the strategic repositioning of firms in the Cambridge Services Index (Figure 2–4). Note the multiple interventions of one industry group into another as firms vie for competitive advantage.

Boundaries shift in any industry when suppliers integrate forward, when customers integrate backward, or when competitors integrate vertically. Industry boundaries are altered as well by technology, for

Figure 2–4.   Strategic Positioning of Firms in the Cambridge Services Index.

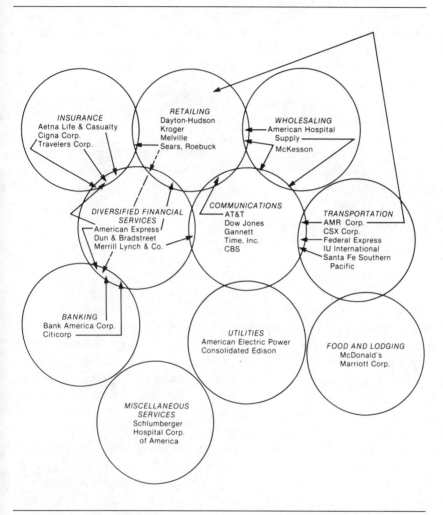

Source: James L. Heskett, *Managing in the Service Economy* (Boston: Harvard Business School Press, 1986). Reprinted by permission.

example when a new technology, such as solar energy, begins to displace mature technology, such as fossil fuel energy. Does the manufacture and sale of solar energy systems represent a new industry or simply an embryonic product line within an existing industry? These decisions must be made with careful regard for the dynamics of competition and the changes in the market. The introduction of digital technology to the calculator industry, for example, opened the vast new market of users of hand calculators.

The distinction between world or global industries, and multidomestic, national, or regional industries also merits attention. In global industries, world competitors strive to serve homogeneous markets with standardized products (wheat, photographic film, and semiconductors are obvious current examples), and new global industries continue to emerge. The parochial outlook of U.S. automobile and electronics firms in the 1960s allowed Japanese firms to establish strong footholds in industries that ultimately demanded global competition. The moral is clear: If regional or local markets are the primary target for the firm and its competitors, the industry should be viewed as regional or local. But if global competitors are attempting to stake out a position in several markets, a global industry may be imminent, even if the business operates only on a local scale today.

SUMMARY

The practical strategist begins developing strategy by carefully examining alternative ways to organize the firm's activities and to identify the industries in which they compete. Positioning the business in the right industry has an important effect on strategy formulation. If the industry is defined too broadly, the resources of the firm will be dispersed. If the industry definition is too parochial, on the other hand, the business may overlook important market segments or fierce potential competitors.

The corporation facing problems of unmanageable diversity often finds relief in the recognition that its products or organization units can be grouped into a relatively small number of businesses. General Electric in 1968, for example, was able to establish 45 strategic business units (SBUs) from its array of 173 divisions and departments, while Westinghouse has consolidated its business array to 28 units. The more than 50,000 products of 3M now reside in only 19 strategic business centers (SBCs), and Xerox's broad range of document management products and financial services are grouped today into 26 product development units (PDUs).

Needless to say, defining the size and configuration of business units in a corporation is not a theoretical exercise; the ultimate definition is tempered by the organization's history and managerial resources.

In addition, trade-offs are inevitable between the merits of defining large business units in order to maximize efficiency as opposed to defining smaller business units that can be more responsive to market needs.

NOTES

1.   Other forces have also encouraged more precise industry and business definition, as witness the Financial Accounting Standards Board's emphasis on business segment reporting.

3 ANALYZING THE COMPETITIVE ENVIRONMENT

Before developing strategy, business managers often analyze their strengths and weaknesses. But the practical strategist looks first outside the business at the industry, the markets, and the competition. Business strengths and weaknesses are meaningful only in the context of what is happening in the environment, what the market seeks, and how the competitors are positioned.

ASSESSING THE INDUSTRY

Several recent techniques for organizing information about an industry are helpful. The most useful are based on the concepts of industry structure and industry maturity.

Understanding Industry Structure

An industry is part of an input/output system, as illustrated in Figure 3–1. The industry transforms or adds value to raw materials provided as input by suppliers. The products or services of the industry constitute the output to the market. If the industry as a whole is strong relative to suppliers or customers, it tends to be profitable (provided, of course,

Figure 3–1. Industry Structure.

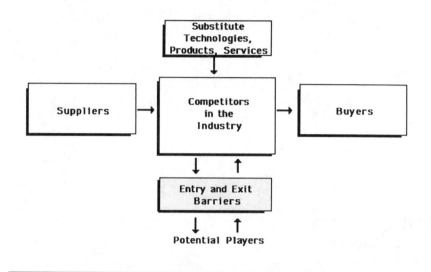

that new competition does not have easy access to the market, or the customer does not have numerous acceptable substitutes). The relative performance of any single competitor is determined by how large an advantage it can establish relative to suppliers, customers, or other competitors.

Needless to say, managers prefer to compete in industries that have long-term profit potential, and certain industries exhibit greater profitability than others. Table 3–1 lists the 10 most profitable U.S. industries during the five-year period 1983–1987. The median performance (return on equity) of U.S. firms across all industries during this period was 12.8 percent, although some industries earned only meager returns, as exemplified by the negative return on equity in the steel industry.

Corporations having excess resources often consider diversifying into a more profitable industry. For many corporations already doing business in an industry, however, diversification is an academic issue if exit barriers prohibit them from shifting assets. Escaping from the industry may not be possible without paying a heavy price. Corporations also find that significant barriers inhibit their entry to other, more attractive industries. As a result, most managers are destined to play out the hands they were dealt.

Table 3-1. Industry Profitability, 1983-87.

Rank	Industry	ROE (5-Year Average %)
1	Beverages and tobacco	20.5
2	Communications media	19.1
3	Financial services	18.7
4	Industrial, office services	18.1
5	Health	17.5
6	Electrical equipment	16.3
7	Food processors	16.3
8	Retailing	16.1
9	Food distributors	16.1
10	Electric utilities	14.4

Source: "Who's Where in the Industry Groups," *Forbes*, January 11, 1988, pp. 224–225.

For these managers, a careful study of industry structure can provide vivid insights into how to manage more effectively. Even in an industry exhibiting poor average profitability, an individual business can excel if it achieves or maintains competitive advantage.

Details of Industry Structure[1]

Supplier Behavior.   The performance of competitors in any industry remains depressed if they lack control over raw material cost or supply. This can occur when any of the following conditions prevails:

Few Suppliers.   Buyers are fragmented relative to suppliers, and the buyers constitute a small fraction of the suppliers' sales. Labor falls into this category if it is highly organized.

Differentiated Suppliers.   Suppliers' products are differentiated or switching costs are high. The fewer the alternative suppliers, the greater the buyers' disadvantage.

Forward Integration.   Suppliers threaten to integrate forward, becoming competitors in the industry they now supply.

Customer Behavior.   Buyers or customers tend to be strong relative to their suppliers (the industry) under certain circumstances:

Few Customers.   Markets characterized by few customers (the defense market, for example), are notoriously unattractive to prospective suppliers, especially if sales to individual customers are large relative to a supplier's sales volume; a fragmented market offers suppliers greater opportunity to establish an advantage.

Undifferentiated Products or Services.   To the degree that customers have many options (or need pay only a small premium to switch) they gain power relative to suppliers. Similar power is ceded to customers if the suppliers' product is not an important part of the customers' value chain.

Backward Integration.   Customers who could reasonably integrate backward inhibit the tendency of suppliers to raise prices. For tire manufacturers, for example, the threat of automobile firms' manufacturing their own tires constrains profitability.

Many Substitute Products.   Above a given threshold of price, quality, service, or other attribute, customers seek a substitute for the industry's product, one that can perform the same function. Examples of substitutability include aluminum for steel, wine for beer, airplane travel for train travel, solar energy for fossil energy. The incentive to switch is often high price, but social values and norms are influential as well (as in the substitution of fish for meat, saccharin for sugar, soft drinks for beer and wine).

Rivalry within the Industry.   Intense and sometimes bitter rivalry among competitors can be found in industries that exhibit certain conditions:

Many Competitors.   Competition is intense when the industry is fragmented (or is populated by a few well-matched players), particularly if the industry is growing slowly.

High Fixed Costs.   When fixed costs are high relative to variable costs, firms are under pressure to use more capacity, most often by attempting to gain share. This fosters price wars that benefit none of the competitors. Industries in which firms add capacity in large increments display the same behavior.

Undifferentiated Products.   For commodity products or services, price competition is typically the deciding purchase factor. Unless switching costs for the customer are high, margins decline for all competitors, and the industry becomes stalemated, with none of the competitors profitable.

High Stakes.   If the financial or strategic rewards for winning are perceived to be large, competitors will be loath to depart the industry, especially if the exit barriers are high.

Exit Barriers.   Not only is the immediate cost of abandoning fixed assets or inventory a barrier to exit, but the delayed cost of satisfying customer obligations is also an obstacle to withdrawal. An economic analysis must consider how to absorb corporate costs that are borne by potential discontinued operations. In a number of European countries, withdrawal from an industry is costly because of the government requirement to provide continuing economic security for workers. And in many corporations, loss of face is a powerful disincentive to throwing in the towel.

Ultimately the attractiveness of an industry will be determined by how much value it creates for customers and, more important, how much of the added value competitors are able to retain. No one profits when competition is so fierce that no firm or group of firms is able to sustain competitive advantage. Such stalemated industry is unattractive both to new entrants and existing players.

Entry Barriers. It is not surprising, as other research has shown, that profitable businesses are often shielded from new competition by high entry barriers to the industry. These usually take several forms:

Capital Requirements. The need for large amounts of capital is obvious when major investments in plant or equipment are a prerequisite even to entering the fray. The cost deters small entrepreneurs from entry. Although large entrepreneurial corporations may have access to large amounts of capital, their effective cost of capital may be higher than the capital cost for the early, smaller entrants, because of the higher risk. And even major corporations are prone to underestimate the total entry fee, as exemplified by RCA and GE during their ill-fated foray into the computer industry in the 1960s.

Economies of Scale. Although economies of scale are often assumed to apply to manufacturing, they can be found in any functional area or activity. Thus, in the brewing industry, scale economies in advertising give Anheuser-Busch significant edge over small regional players; in the information processing industry, IBM realizes comparable economies in R&D. Corporations who are able to share resources across their businesses gain an additional edge, a situation addressed under field analysis.

Product Differentiation. The implication of entering an industry characterized by differentiated or branded products is that customers must be persuaded to switch to new products. The cost of reestablishing customer loyalty represents an entry barrier for new competitors.

Distribution Channels. Access to distribution channels represents a major obstacle to entry, particularly in mature industries. Beverage and tobacco, drugs, food products, and many other consumer goods industries exhibit these barriers. Occasionally a new channel can be devised, as witness the recent success of direct television marketing, but this is unusual and may prove to be a fad.

Other Cost Barriers.   Cost advantage also derives from easy access to cheap labor, capital (for example a government subsidy or tax advantage), or raw material, including energy. Favorable locations (proximity to customers or suppliers) provide cost advantages to early entrants. And patented or proprietary technology offers still further cost benefits.

Government Policy.   Awards of monopolistic licenses (as in the hypermarket industry in France), or for that matter the assumption of a monopolistic position by the government itself (the 1981 takeover by the French government of chemical and aluminum industries) inhibits new entrants. Subtler deterrence can come from government licensing standards and policies (exemplified by the seven-year period of testing required before the U.S. Food and Drug Administration [FDA] approves a new pharmaceutical in this country.)

Expected Retaliation.   A powerful psychological barrier to entry arises if existing firms are committed to holding their positions and have substantial resources with which to defend themselves against intruders. This situation occurs frequently in capital-intensive industries experiencing slow growth.

Analyzing Industry Life Cycle

The *product* life cycle is familiar to most managers. Products are introduced, they experience increased demand, and then fall into relative disuse. Hula hoops, bamboo rakes, buggy whips, parachutes, church pews, and horseshoes illustrate this phenomenon. Although the *industry* life cycle is less well appreciated, this concept provides managers with the additional dimension required to understand the dynamics of industry structure. The premise in this model is that entire industries, like products and markets, also evolve through a life cycle (Figure 3–2). During this cycle industry structure undergoes major transformation. The life cycle can last for just a few months or extend for many years.

Life Cycle Stages.   Although the number of stages is arbitrary, it is convenient to divide the life cycle into four stages. Table 3–2 provides examples of industries in the various stages of maturity.

The individual stages typically exhibit unequal length whose duration depends on the industry. Industries may abide in a particular stage

Figure 3–2. Industry Life Cycle.

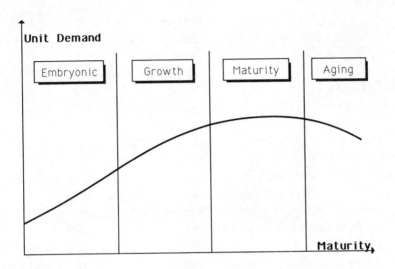

Table 3–2. Examples of Industry Maturity.

Embryonic Stage

Artificial intelligence
Genetic engineering
Holography
Lasers

Solar energy
Space travel
Superconductivity

Growth Stage

Cable TV
Consumer electronics
Fiber optics
Minicomputers and PCs

Robotics
Semiconductors
VCRs

Mature Stage

Chemicals
Mainframe computers
Motion picture theaters
Natural resources (some)
Plastics (some)
Textiles

Sporting goods
  Hang gliding (embryonic)
  Wind surfing (growth)
  Tennis (mature)
  Baseball (aging)

Late Mature or Aging Stage

Automobiles
Bakeries
Beer
Candy
Distilled spirits
Greeting cards
Men's hats

Nuclear power
Railroad passenger travel
Restaurants
Shipbuilding
Shoes
Tires
Tobacco

for many years (holography has been embryonic since 1946, while textiles have been mature since the nineteenth century). Some industries or industry segments on the other hand, like nuclear power, pass quickly through many stages. Tennis boomed in the 1970s. But since 1979, active tennis players are reported to have declined by 40 percent in the United States to 11 million. Equipment sales experienced similar decline. Manufacturers sold 5 million tennis racquets in 1978, but a total of only 2.7 million in 1985.[2]

When a product or service is introduced to a market and an industry begins to emerge, demand may grow rapidly. Total demand in this embryonic stage is small, however, and vacillates substantially. During the growth stage, overall product demand normally increases much faster than the gross national product. As the industry matures, growth slows to approximately that of the GNP. Most industries (and the U.S. economy as a whole) are mature. In the aging stage, demand grows more slowly than GNP and ultimately declines in real terms.

Since any industry by definition comprises all the businesses competing against one another within it, the maturity of an industry defines the maturity of all the businesses within it. Specific market segments within an industry, however, may have different positions on the life cycle. Maturities in the sporting goods industry, for example, range across the spectrum. The declining market for baseball bats is served by only a few competitors, while the burgeoning market for windsurfers is served by a large number of competitors. The market for color television is mature in the United States, growing in Europe, and embryonic in South America. Thus, although a business cannot escape its industry, it can improve position relative to the other competitors by focusing on high growth segments.

Product demand is the most obvious indicator of maturity. The assessment may be biased, however, if one considers only the quantitative dimensions of maturity. Table 3–3 summarizes some of the qualitative factors, including the potential demand for the product and the characteristics of the competitors and customers. These major variables change stage by stage:

Embryonic Stage. In the early stages of an industry, the growth rate is rapid and erratic, although unit sales may be quite small. Potential is hard to define accurately, because customer needs are only beginning to evolve. The number of competitors also is unpredictable, although the industry is easy to enter. Investment is low (many embryonic industries originate as cottage businesses), but variable costs are high.

Table 3–3. Guide to Industry Maturity.

| Factor | Embryonic | Maturity Stage | | |
		Growth	Mature	Aging
1. Growth Rate	Normally much greater than GNP (on small base).	Sustained growth above GNP. New customers. New suppliers. Rate decelerates toward end of stage.	Approximately equals GNP.	Declining demand. Market shrinks as users' needs change.
2. Predictability of growth potential	Hard to define accurately. Small portion of demand being satisfied. Market forecasts differ widely.	Greater percentage of demand is met and upper limits of demand becoming clearer. Discontinuities, such as price reductions based on economies of scale, may occur.	Potential well defined. Competition specialized to satisfy needs of specific segments.	Known and limited.
3. Product line proliferation	Specialized lines to meet needs of early customers.	Rapid expansion.	Proliferation slows or ceases.	Lines narrow as unprofitable products dropped.
4. Number of Competitors	Unpredictable.	Reaches maximum. New entrants attracted by growth and high margins. Some consolidation begins toward end of stage.	Entrenched positions established. Further shakeout of marginal competitors.	New entrants unlikely. Competitors continue to decline.
5. Market share distribution	Unstable. Shares react unpredictably to entrepreneurial insights and timing.	Increasing stability. Typically, a few competitors emerging as strong.	Stable, with a few companies often controlling much of industry.	Highly concentrated or fragmented if industry segments.
6. Customer stability	Trial usage with little customer loyalty.	Some loyalty. Repeat usage with many seeking alternative suppliers.	Well-developed buying patterns with customer loyalty. Competitors understand purchase dynamics and it is difficult for a new supplier to win over accounts.	Extremely stable. Suppliers dwindle and customers less motivated to seek alternatives.
7. Ease of entry	Normally easy. No one dominates. Customers' expectations uncertain. If barriers exist, they are usually technology, capital, or fear of the unknown.	More difficult. Market franchises and/or economies of scale may exist, yet new business is still available without directly confronting competiton.	Difficult. Market leaders established. New business must be "won" from others.	Little or no incentive to enter.
8. Technology	Plays an important role in matching product characteristics to market needs. Frequent product changes.	Product technology vital early, while process technology more important later in this stage.	Process and material substitution focus. Product requirements well known and relatively undemanding. May be a thrust to renew the industry via new technology.	Technological content is known, stable, and accessible.

Market share distribution is volatile, fluctuating among various competitors. This instability is fostered by the uncertain expectations of customers who seek products or services on a trial basis with little loyalty to suppliers. Suppliers seek to satisfy special customer requirements by adapting and furthering the technology to match product characteristics to market needs. As a result, product modification is common.

Growth Stage.   Overall unit and dollar growth increases rapidly in the growth stage as new customers discover the product. Toward the end of this stage, however, the rate of growth declines and becomes more predictable.

Attracted by market growth and visions of profit, competitors increase to a maximum number, although the increasing capital intensity of the industry eliminates some early entrants. Shakeout and consolidation characterize the late growth stages as competitive pressures increase (for example, because of price reductions based on economies of scale).

As competitors accumulate market franchises and secure market share, new players find it harder to enter. The risk of entry diminishes, of course, if share can be gained without a direct attack on existing competitors, for example by finding customers with special needs. Although loyalty to suppliers is increasing, many customers continue to seek alternative suppliers. A few businesses may control a large fraction of industry sales, and market share begins to stabilize. The product line proliferates rapidly during the growth stage, and product technology continues to be a critical basis for competition in most industries.

Mature Stage.   At maturity, the industry grows at approximately the growth rate of the economy. At least 75 percent of the assets of U.S. corporations are found in mature industries, including most primary materials sectors (metals, forest products, oil) and much secondary manufacturing. The potential for growth is well defined in this stage, and the industry behaves in a fairly predictable manner, although cyclicity often reflects imbalances of supply and demand.

The number of competitors is stable (although competitors are eliminated if their costs are too high), and market share changes very slowly. An oligopoly often exists in which a few competitors claim most of the industry revenues (as in automobiles and energy). Many firms attempt to satisfy specialized market requirements, finding a niche by differentiation. Entry to the industry during this stage is difficult, because economies of scale favor entrenched competitors, and significant share cannot be obtained from the growth of the market. Customers are stable and buying patterns are well established.

Technology continues to be important. But since significant new product features are rarely demanded by the market, the technological focus shifts toward materials improvement and process efficiency. As a consequence, product proliferation usually stops in the late mature stage of the industry, as the recovery of product development expenditures becomes more difficult.

Aging Stage.   Industries age when demand for products or services begins to decline, often when the industry can no longer satisfy fully the changing needs of the market. Many competitors adopt rationalization strategies in this stage, withdrawing from unprofitable markets and eliminating marginal products.

As the number of competitors declines by withdrawal or consolidation, the market share of remaining competitors increases. Share distribution becomes more fragmented, however, if competitors attempt to survive by securing a grip on a specific market or product niche.

Stable, long-term relationships between customers and suppliers are an important basis for competition at this stage. Customers have little incentive to seek new sources of supply; their options become fewer in any case as the number of suppliers diminishes. But price sensitivity declines as the importance of product availability increases.

Entry barriers to an aging industry may be low; depressed stock multiples often facilitate entry by acquisition. New competitors are rarely attracted, however, with the exception of those who seek a source of positive cash flow. Investments for technology, either in the form of process improvement or product development, are usually minimal, although innovation may renew the industry.

Aging industries fail to excite the interest of managers who have espoused growth as primary virtue. Neverthelesss, it is important to remember that numerous vintage businesses can be found in aging industries. (Nucor in steel, Brown-Foreman in distilled spirits, Paccor in trucks, and Hallmark in greeting cards represent some of the better known examples.) Thus, even though profit margins for the industry overall are declining, the surviving businesses may be extremely profitable (the last icemen on the block[3]). And indeed, many corporations celebrate their aging businesses as finally returning the investments made in earlier stages of industry maturity.

The Effect of Technology.   Forces within an industry rarely have an effect on industry maturity, with the exception of technological innovation. A classic example is the Japanese abacus industry, which in 1965 produced over 3 million units, the result of slow but steady growth since the device was introduced from China in the sixteenth century. Disaster appeared imminent, however, when the cheap electronic hand calculator was introduced. World sales of pocket and desk calculators amounted to only 4,000 units in 1965, but by 1978 over 40 million units were being sold annually. Abacus output had dropped to two million units, although abacus manufacturers now forecast an annual growth rate of 3 percent. The slide rule industry has not been so fortunate. Sales of over 20,000 units per month in the late 1950s have now declined to fewer than 200 per year.

The explosion of compact disk sales in the record industry provides another example of the dramatic potential impact of technology. From 1984 to 1986, unit sales increased from 6 million to 53 million units, while long-playing disks experienced a 38 percent decline in sales to 125 million units. The watch industry experienced similar transformation when new LED, LCD, and digital technologies were introduced.

One of the most poignant instances of technological trauma can be found in the history of the pony express. Established on April 3, 1860 as the Central Overland California & Pike's Peak Express Company, the pony express delivered mail over a 1,966 mile route from St. Joseph, Missouri to Sacramento, California. But the technological challenge of the electric telegraph was too great to overcome, and the pony express service expired on October 26, 1861—a short and glorious life cycle.

Implications of the Industry Life Cycle.   Maturation alters the characteristics of the industry in which businesses compete, as Table 3–3 demonstrates. We invariably observe, as a consequence, a change in the way businesses compete with one another. In an embryonic industry, for example, price is almost never a basis for competition; customers typically buy on the basis of product features. In a mature industry, on the other hand, price is almost always a basis for competition. As a result, managers need to modify their strategy as their business moves from one stage to another.

As strategy changes, the investment requirements of the business change and so does the financial performance, as illustrated in Figure 3–3. Embryonic businesses almost always lose money initially, as revenue lags cost and expense. Profit turns positive in the growth stage, as does cash flow. As the market matures, revenue levels off, reducing the need for continuing investment. Profit and cash flow both tend to reach their maximum during maturity.

Figure 3–3. Change of Financial Performance with Maturity.

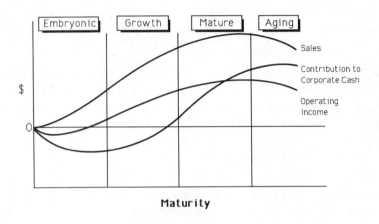

Unlike managers, an industry may not mature inexorably with time. Some industries experience rejuvenation. The ski industry, as one example, was mature until the mid-1950s. Increases in leisure time and heightened interest in physical fitness, coupled with greater consumer affluence, conspired to increase demand. Market activity was fueled by technological developments in skis (wood, replaced by metal, replaced in turn by composite materials), bindings, and boots. Demand was sustained by snowmaking technology that extended the normal season by several months. The mature ski industry of the 1950s became a growth industry in the 1960s and 1970s, and now in the 1980s is once again mature. The bicycle industry of the 1970s enjoyed a comparable revitalization as a result of energy concerns, increased leisure time, and a sudden interest in health and physical fitness. Now, 10 years later, it too is mature.

The notion that most industries inevitably mature is often hard for managers to accept, perhaps because of the vested interest they have in retaining their corporate image or career aspirations. Businesses that consider themselves to be in a growth stage, for example, continue to command corporate investment. Similarly, clinging to a classification of "maturity" shields managers from having to cope with the trauma of consolidation during the aging stage. From an economic point of view, however, no stage has greater value than any other. Businesses

in the embryonic and growth stages represent the future of the corporation, but they demand high investment and often entail major risks.
Well-managed mature and vintage businesses generate high profit and
substantial cash, thus permitting the expansion of businesses in earlier
stages of maturity, even though their own growth potential is limited.

Other Industry Factors

The popular treatments of the future by Alvin Toffler and John Naisbitt
reflect the substantial amount of time and energy devoted to discerning
emerging trends and their probable impact on society.[4] While many
of their forecasts have failed to materialize, they do focus managerial
attention on possible future scenarios, a subject addressed in depth
in the chapter on corporate strategy.

A manager in any business needs to identify the critical factors that
determine the performance and future behavior of the firm. Some conditions influence only specific industries. For example, the aging of
the population bodes well for the eyewear business; 60 percent of the
U.S. population already wears glasses or contact lenses. The safety razor
industry emerged, as Peter Drucker observes, because of men's need
to look neat, the increasing cost of personal barbers, the risk of straight
razors, and the time required to get shaved in a barbershop.

While it is important to be cognizant of the broad shifts occurring
in society, the manager must also pay close attention to the conditions
that directly affect his own industry. A checklist of other important
variables follows:

- *Factors affecting growth.* What factors have the greatest positive
  or negative impact on industry performance? These include both
  general economic conditions and specific social, political, legal,
  and demographic changes.
- *Product breadth.* Is product breadth an important competitive
  factor? Do most competitors have broad or narrow product lines?
  Do products have a high or low level of differentiation, and how
  are they differentiated (product features, performance, packaging, price)?
- *Technology.* What role does technology play in the industry? Is
  R&D declining or intensifying? Is it product oriented or process
  oriented?
- *Vertical integration.* Are industry participants integrating? If so,
  in what direction (vertical or horizontal)? What benefits in scale
  or scope derive from vertical integration, and how are these
  benefits translated into competitive advantage?

- *Profitability.* What is the average profitability of the industry? Is there wide or narrow dispersion among participants, market segments, or distribution channels? Is profitability increasing or decreasing, and what inferences may be drawn from the operating characteristics of firms at each end of the spectrum?
- *Critical issues.* What are the critical issues that face the industry? Are all participants affected equally, or are some insulated by product or geographic focus or relationship to suppliers?

Managers having this kind of information can not only identify the trends influencing the business, but develop strategies to defend against or capitalize on the trends to ensure the competitive viability of the firm.

ASSESSING THE MARKET

Despite the wealth of popular and academic literature devoted to marketing theory, research, and analysis, and the remarkable amount of data available to managers from sales and operations reports or even the general press, few managers understand their markets. Even fewer, unfortunately, can translate market data into practical strategy. The factors contributing to this dolorous condition are varied:

- Too few data are available.
- Too much data is available (overburdening the manager's capacity to select the relevant information).
- The wrong data are used to predict market activity.
- The right data are misinterpreted.

A paucity of data is most unusual, except in emerging industries, and it is extraordinary that a manager cannot collect sufficient data on the characteristics of the market. More commonly, managers are overwhelmed by the breadth and detail of the data base. Their own customers represent the most important source of market intelligence. As a result, the first recourse of any manager who needs more data is to review the methods and frequency of direct customer contact used by the business. Many managers underestimate the willingness of customers to talk about their business with a valued supplier, particularly if the end result is an improvement in product or service quality.

We have defined the market as the set of customers served by the industry, the set of all the competitors. Even the leading firm in an industry, however, rarely serves the entire market, although it may hold a strong position in many segments. For any business, therefore, the important questions are: Which segments of the markets shall we serve? and What are the customer needs in these segments? The answers to these two queries will provide critical input to the manager who seeks effective strategies: competitive advantage in its simplest expression means no more than satisfying customers better than do the competitors.

Defining Market Segments

What is the most appropriate way to segment the market? A number of possibilities present themselves, including

- Segment size and growth rate
- Geography
- Product type
- Distribution channel
- Customer type
- Customer need (application)

Sales or product shipment data are usually available by geography, product type, and channel in all but the newest industries. Other than providing a general context for analyzing market behavior, however, these data are less valuable strategically than data on customer type (demographic or psychographic) or customer need; understanding customer purchase criteria is the prerequisite to serving any segment effectively.

The most useful segmentation scheme recognizes key similarities in needs within groups of customers and key differences in needs between those groups. The differences between groups, moreover, should be profound enough to yield opportunities to differentiate products or services from competitors' products. Examples of firms who have applied this segmentation logic include the following:

General Cinema.   GC pioneered the concept of small movie theaters in shopping malls. These theaters, usually with two to four screens, responded specifically to the entertainment needs of customers in suburban and rural locations, providing both convenience (location) and a broad selection (multiple screens).

Crown Cork & Seal.   As a competitor in the commodity container industry dominated by American Can, Continental, and National, Crown Cork & Seal fared poorly. By withdrawing to high-growth specialty segments such as beverage and aerosol cans, and emphasizing customer responsiveness, Crown was able to realize the highest profit margins in the industry.

Honda.   By introducing small recreational motorcycles, Honda was able to address the educational and transportation needs of a new market segment. The market had been dominated historically by British firms (BSA and Triumph) and U.S. companies such as Harley-Davidson that produced large, powerful machines for professional sports enthusiasts and bikers. Its overall market position today certifies Honda as the industry leader.

Allegheny Ludlum Steel.   This firm has dedicated all its resources to the specialty steel segment of the steel industry. Supported by a vigorous program of restructuring and cost reduction, the firm's concentration on stainless and silicon electric steels has produced rapid growth in mature markets. Return on equity of 19 percent in 1987 was far greater than the average for large competitors serving many markets.

Defining segments based upon customer needs is a difficult process, particularly for consumer products where the basis of segmentation may include not only tangible attributes (specific features, functions, or applications), but also customer demographics (age, sex, location), and psychographics (image, ego reinforcement). Industrial product manufacturers often have an easier task of segmenting based on needs, as customers frequently provide detailed or unique product specifications. Nevertheless, opportunities still exist for industrial product firms to segment based on service attributes such as financing, delivery, or repair and maintenance. Several firms, including GE and Xerox, have successfully segmented industrial markets based on the intensity of customer needs for service, and then differentiated from competitors on the basis of service quality.

Once the market segments have been defined and the customer needs identified, the additional data requirements are straightforward. Managers must be able to characterize the size and growth of key segments. The skyline chart in Figure 3–4 for the U.S. packaging industry offers a graphic way to compare the size and growth of different segments.

Growth criteria must be specified carefully. *Unit sales* of tobacco, as an example, have declined slowly; U.S. consumption in 1986 declined to 584 billion cigarettes, continuing the 1.9 percent compound annual decrease since 1981. *Per capita consumption* declined even faster: 3,277 cigarettes per capita in 1986, down from 4,092 per capita in 1976. But *dollar revenues* in the industry continued to grow, largely

Figure 3–4. Packaging Industry Segments.

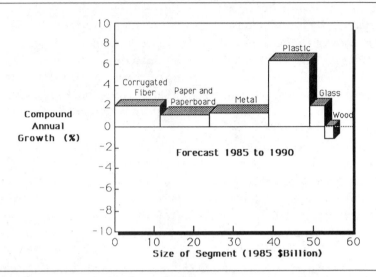

the result of price increases (7 percent in both 1985 and 1986). And even in a declining market, some segments have shown growth. Use of snuff, for example, increased steadily from 1972 to 1985.

Managers should also be able to identify the trends in the following:

- Distribution channels and patterns
- Price structure and movement
- Import and export levels
- Market cyclicity or seasonality
- Advertising and promotion practices

This information reveals to the practical strategist how the market is evolving and provides guidance on strategy formulation.

Interpreting Market Data

Astute managers strive to look beyond the simple display of market statistics to understand the forces responsible for changes in market growth and size. An inflection in market demand is often the result of a change in external factors such as government legislation, social values, or economic conditions. Regulation or deregulation of an industry usually has a profound effect on maturity. The nuclear power industry moved rapidly from the growth stage in the 1960s to virtual extinction in the 1980s as the result of regulation, while the telecommunications, banking, and airlines industries were rejuvenated by deregulation.

Changes in the environment often produce a cascade of market effects. Consider the Organization of Petroleum Exporting Countries (OPEC) oil cartel, which in October 1973 began to manipulate world oil prices. The free market price of $2.41 per barrel of crude oil escalated to $10.95 by the beginning of 1974 and subsequently was raised to $37 before market pressures began to assert themselves and prices began to fall. As a result, in the automobile industry, consumers turned to compact cars (in spite of the skepticism of U.S. manufacturers). The tire industry was hit with the one-two punch of smaller cars and reduced driving, both of which reduced tire consumption sharply, while new radial technology simultaneously increased tire longevity. The sparkplug industry suffered as well, from the introduction of cars having fewer cylinders. But the smaller cars were salutary, on the other hand, for manufacturers of luggage racks, whose sales soared by more than 50 percent.

Similar benefits from the energy crisis were experienced by producers of chain saws, a third of whose sales were diverted to harvesting wood, and log splitters. Wood stove sales expanded with equal vigor until users wearied of cutting wood to stoke the stove and antipollution legislation materialized to stem the clouds of smoke.

A business can rarely serve all the markets that are theoretically available to it. To begin with, unless the industry is in its early stages, the needs of customers in different segments vary. As a result, serving every segment demands resources that exceed the capability of most organizations. Furthermore, a business normally achieves greater success by concentrating on segments in which it has advantages relative to the competition.

As a general rule, small, rapidly growing segments are more attractive than large, stable segments already populated with tenacious competitors. In the beverage industry, for example, the high-growth segments such as bottled water can accommodate a host of competitors; large slow-growth segments such as coffee tend to be dominated by a few large competitors. Whenever possible, small firms need to seek attractive niches, that is, segments that are defensible against rapacious intruders and cheaper to serve than other segments.

Figure 3–5.   Perceptual Map—Brand Images.

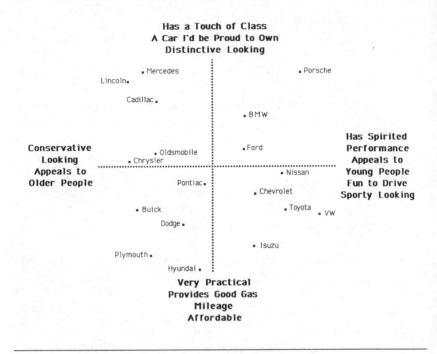

Source: Chrysler Corp. Adapted with permission.

The quality of market analysis also determines the success of product positioning. A common tool for identifying positioning opportunities is the perceptual map. Such maps display the customer perceptions of the various competitors and their products in terms of key purchasing criteria. Figure 3–5, for example, updates Chrysler's analysis of the 1984 automobile market. Although the utility of a perceptual map depends strongly on the careful selection of the attributes to be mapped, it can yield valuable insights into how to differentiate products.

In many markets customers place a high priority on *value*, the level of product quality they get for a given price. The concept of quality is usually taken to include all product attributes (including service) other than price. The importance of quality explains why Maytag is able to realize a $150 premium from its image of reliability, and Frank Perdue benefits from 10 cents per pound premium for his "fresh" chickens.

But competitors may deliberately position their products in different ways. They may provide equal value by selling a premium product at

Figure 3–6. The Price/Quality Relationship.

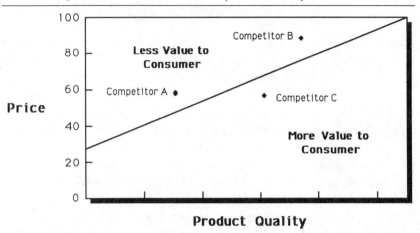

Product Quality

a high price (competitor B in the example of Figure 3–6) or an economy product at a low price (competitor A in the example). In the automobile industry, for example, General Motors positions its product line along the entire range of value, with Cadillac as the premium product, Chevrolet as the economy product, and Buick, Pontiac, and Oldsmobile in the middle range. Discount merchandisers typically position themselves at the low end of the range (at or below point A in Figure 3–6) against department stores at the upper end of the range.

The relationship between quality and price in a market is described by the diagonal or *fair value* line; in markets served by unique or high-risk products (for example, cardiovascular drugs), value is strongly dependent upon quality, whereas in markets served by commodity products, value depends strongly on price. The fair value relationship often shifts to the right as competitors introduce new technology or reduce price to gain market share.

Competitors who position themselves below the fair value line are perceived by the customer as offering greater value (higher quality at an equivalent price or equivalent quality at lower price) and can expect to gain share. Conversely, the competitor who offers lower value can expect to lose share. The strategic imperatives of low value relative to competitors are straightforward: Either improve quality or cut price. Similarly, a competitor whose products are highly valued may increase price or simply allow market share to increase as customers switch to products having higher value for them.

ASSESSING THE COMPETITION

Strategy demands that businesses deploy their resources toward market opportunities in a way that distinguishes them from their competitors. It follows that analysis of competitors is a crucial precursor to the formulation of good strategy. Nonetheless, such analysis is often implicit or incomplete or lacking objectivity. Managers often assume that they know all about the competition and do not have to waste time on further analysis, that the information cannot be collected, or that competitors cannot be evaluated. Analyzing competitors is indeed time consuming, and collecting information may be difficult, particularly if it is not available in the public domain.

Despite these impediments, almost every company is capable of good analysis of the competition, and some excel, as evidenced by their timely response to threats or anticipation of challenges. Good analysis includes assessment of competitors' relative strengths and weaknesses and of their strategy, performance, and commitment to the business.

Examination of competitors' current product, pricing, distribution, and marketing practice can reveal their strategies and should also include prediction of how the competitors might act in the future. Prediction includes hypothesizing how the competitors will respond both to changes in the external environment and to changes in the analyst's own possible strategies.

The current performance of each competitor should be reviewed with respect to sales, growth, market share, profit margin, net income, return on investment, and cash flow. The historical performance of a competitor serves as a good indicator of goals in the marketplace. A final component of competition analysis is identifying those businesses that might become competitors. Potential competitors include firms who may define their markets or products differently. Firms farther up or down the value chain may integrate and transform themselves from suppliers and distributors to forceful competitors as well.

Value Chain Analysis

The activities of any business consist in adding value to materials purchased from suppliers. The term *value added* is usually defined as the price of the product or service minus the cost of purchased materials. When expressed in terms of a ratio to sales, capital investment, or number of employees, it serves as a useful measure of productivity. Profit Impact of Market Strategy (PIMS) data suggest that return on investment is favorably affected by an increase in value added (see Chapter 4).

A thorough competitive analysis demands that the practical strategist understand the value chain, for an analysis of how value is added can provide two important pieces of competitive intelligence.

First, where in the chain is the greatest value added? This will suggest how managerial attention should be allocated. More payoff will be realized from a 1 percent improvement in a high-value element of the chain than from a 10 percent improvement in a trivial element.

Second, in which segments of the chain do competitors have a competitive edge? Their advantages or disadvantages in the value chain will reflect differences both in strategy and efficiency.

For example, a firm distributing through conventional channels may incur distribution costs equal to 5–10 percent of sales; when direct marketing techniques are employed, distribution costs may be 20–25 percent of sales. Similarly, a technology leader may incur R&D expenses equal to 10 percent of sales while the technology follower spends only 5 percent of sales on R&D.

When the strategy of two firms is apparently identical, then differences in the value chain are evidence of different efficiencies. If these are rooted in implementation problems, remedial measures can be taken. If the differences are the result of economies of scale, however, the problem is more serious.

Table 3–4 contrasts the value chain for two businesses operating at constant volume. Business A achieves higher margins as a result of its lower manufacturing cost. But because business B is able to realize comparable margins with lower investment, its profitability (return on capital employed) is higher.

Field Analysis

Corporations having businesses that overlap in one or more functional dimension realize competitive advantages; these occur within the realm of product development, manufacturing, marketing, or distribution. The concept of strategic field was introduced to address the role of these shared resources or linkages in reducing cost or improving efficiency.

Table 3–4. The Value Chain.

Price/Unit	100%	100%
Value-added steps		
Materials	40	40
Manufacturing	30	35
Distribution	10	6
Marketing	5	6
R&D	3	6
Administration	4	2
Cost/Unit	92	95
Profit/Unit	8	5
Assets	40	20
Return on net assets	20%	25%

Field analysis attempts to determine the source and magnitude of these advantages. Consider the example of Georgia-Pacific, a commodity-based corporation that has achieved strong competitive position as a result of its field strength.[5] According to field analysis theory, Georgia-Pacific's strength in raw materials, distribution, and chemical manufacturing allows it to grow and prosper in several businesses even though it may not be the leader in any one business.

Examples of other corporations that gain competitive advantage from field strength include Warner-Lambert, General Electric, IBM, and Procter and Gamble. We can conclude generally that corporations who manage a set of unrelated businesses may suffer relative to those who manage a set of related businesses, an idea expanded upon later in the discussion of diversification.

Market Share

Market share is often viewed as an important *determinant* of competitive strength, although it may also be the *result* of competitive strength. Size in itself is not a good measure of strength: Chrysler is larger than Procter and Gamble, but P&G holds a strong position in its industry whereas Chrysler is relatively weak. Market share is a much better measure of competitive position.

Share is defined in several ways. A common method is to look at the dollar value of sales:

Market share = Business sales ($)/Total market sales ($).

In commodities industries where most competitors sell most products at the same or similar price, this definition is useful, although it may obscure the importance of price, since Sales = Price * Unit Volume. As a result, an alternative definition is often preferred:

Market share = Business sales (units)/Total market sales (units).

Absolute measures of market share may be misleading, however, since even 5 percent share can give a competitor a commanding position if the industry is fragmented. For this reason, measures of relative market share may be better. Two definitions of relative share are in common usage:

Relative market share = Business unit sales/Leading competitor sales.

This definition is customarily used in constructing the Boston Consulting Group (BCG) matrix. An alternative definition is used in PIMS analysis:

Relative market share = Business unit sales/Combined sales of three largest competitors.

A meaningful definition of share pertains only to the market served by the business. For example, although IBM's field strength gave it a strong position in computer hardware overall, its primary stength lies in large, general purpose computers (mainframes), where in 1982 it held almost 70 percent share. But in small business computers the IBM share was only 34 percent, in personal computers its share was 11 percent, and in minicomputers only 3 percent.

In many industries, competitive advantage accrues to businesses having large market share and the resulting economies of scale, and profitability is often proportional to market share. PIMS data, for example, indicate that businesses having greater than 40 percent share earn a pretax return on investment (ROI) greater than 30 percent; businesses having less than 10 percent share earn an average of only 13.2 percent. In a specific example, margins during the 1970s for GM had been significantly higher than for the other U.S. players. But AMC's performance surpassed Chrysler's, a result of its focus on small or four-wheel drive vehicles, compared to the Chrysler full-line strategy. Market share,

Figure 3–7. The Supply Curve.

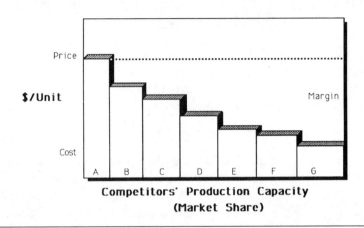

Price

$/Unit   Margin

Cost

A   B   C   D   E   F   G

Competitors' Production Capacity
(Market Share)

of course, is not the only determinant of profitability; relative quality and level of investment are two of the other important variables.

Supply curves represent another way of presenting the effect of market share. These curves, an extension of experience curve theory, are useful in industries such as commodity chemicals in which cost depends strongly upon utilization of capacity. As illustrated in Figure 3–7, the highest share (highest production capacity) competitor achieves the lowest cost and therefore the highest margins. The slope of the supply curve is a function of how much scale or market share affects cost; a steep slope is indicative of strong economies of scale.

Profit and cash flow do not always depend strongly on market share, even if there are economies of scale. The relationship is weak if the added value is low (distribution businesses, for example), if the competition has low-cost sources of supply or better technology, or if more or less capacity is used than competitors are using. Some industries, such as banks, hospitals, and hotels, even exhibit diseconomies of scale. Supermarkets represent an excellent example; regional chains with revenues of less than about $8 billion appear to perform better than larger, national chains.

To summarize, in most situations a business that holds a large share of its served market can expect to be more profitable than its competitors. Moreover, businesses that establish a strong market position early are difficult to dislodge (Table 3–5)[6], although high-share businesses tend to lose share over a period of time. Nevertheless, managers

Table 3–5. Long Live the King.

Category	Leading Brand in 1923	Rank in 1986
Bacon	Swift	First
Cameras	Kodak	First
Canned fruit	Del Monte	First
Canned milk	Carnation	First
Chewing gum	Wrigley	First
Chocolates	Hershey	Second
Flour	Gold Medal	First
Mint candies	Life Savers	First
Paint	Sherwin Williams	First
Pipe tobacco	Prince Albert	First
Razors	Gillette	First
Sewing machines	Singer	First
Soap	Ivory	First
Soft drinks	Coca-Cola	First
Soup	Campbell	First
Tea	Lipton	First
Tires	Goodyear	First
Toothpaste	Colgate	Second

Source: Lubliner/Saltz, Inc., New York. Reprinted with permission.

need to recognize that an improvement in market share may be either exorbitantly expensive or not attainable at all, as illustrated by the Miller example in Chapter 5.

Competitive Position

Competitive position is a measure of the strength of a business within its industry. To determine the *relative* competitive position of a business, simply compare it with its peers using the key success factors for the industry, the qualities necessary to overcome the opposition.

The key success factors will vary by industry; some examples follow:

- Product features (personal computers, software)
- Product cost (beer, steel, paper)
- Product quality and performance (consumer electronics, videotape)
- Brand image (toothpaste, soft drinks, designer jeans)
- Customer service (mainframe computers, home appliances)
- On-time delivery (fashion merchandising, most consumer goods)

Empirical evidence has demonstrated that the factors that determine success or failure rarely exceed five; in some embryonic industries only one factor, technology, is important. Furthermore, the key success factors for an industry (the basis for competition) change as the environment in which the business operates changes. In the automobile industry, for example, quality and fuel economy are being displaced by design as a salient basis for competition (price continues to be important, of course).

Careful assessment of the keys to success in the industry ensures that relative competitive position has been determined using the right criteria and that the right strategies are selected. This assessment is best performed by querying managers who understand the industry, surveying customers and suppliers, and studying successful competitors.

Most comparisons of competitive strength are qualitative, with the exceptions of market share and cost. A few also lend themselves to comparisons using indexes, as exemplified by the PIMS index of product quality:

Quality Index = % superior products − % inferior products.

Thus, by estimating the fraction of products or services deemed by the customer to be better or worse than those of the competitors, the strategist can derive a semiquantitative measure of quality.

A measure of *relative* competitive position is not enough, since all competitors may be in perilous straits. It is also helpful to ascertain the *absolute* competitive position of a business, a measure in part of a firm's ability to implement a variety of strategies. The following classification system, developed originally at Arthur D. Little, is often employed:

Leading firms dominate their industry. IBM has occupied this position in the computer industry for many years (although their position is deteriorating). When IBM changes system architecture, software standards, or price, most competitors are forced to follow its lead. Anheuser-Busch has recently achieved leadership in the brewing industry. As the low-cost producer, the firm controls price in the premium and super-premium segments of the beer market. DeBeers is the leader in the diamond industry, controlling as it does over 80 percent of the world's production.

General Motors dominated the automobile industry for many years, until the corporation's insensitivity to consumer needs allowed German and Japanese competitors to erode its lead. A partial recovery of share in the early-1980s was again lost in the mid-1980s. Constant surveillance is the message. U.S. Steel, the dominant player in steel in the 1950s, committed resources to an old technology. Subsequent allocation of corporate resources to diversification amounted to a tacit withdrawal from the industry, allowing aggressive Japanese firms using new technology to take the lead. Montgomery Ward ceded leadership to Sears after World War II by virtue of its decision not to continue store expansion. And RCA's loss of leadership in color television is legendary (as discussed under global strategy).

By definition, an industry can have only one leader. And since leadership is hard to achieve and even harder to maintain, not every industry has a leader, a firm that controls the performance or behavior of other competitors and can implement whatever strategy it chooses. More common is the leaderless industry made up of one or more strong competitors.

Strong competitors have a wide choice of independent strategies that can be adopted without endangering their short-term position; they are relatively invulnerable to the actions of their competitors. In the computer industry, the Digital Equipment Corporation (DEC) satisfies this specification. In the brewing industry, Miller is a strong competitor. Coca-Cola and PepsiCo represent the two strong competitors in the soft drink industry, while GM and Toyota represent strong competitors in automobiles.

Favorable competitors are able to exploit a specific competitive strength, often in a product and market niche. Apple in the computer industry, Coors in the brewing industry, Seven-Up in soft drinks, and Ford occupy favorable competitive positions. Firms in a favorable competitive position have a better than average opportunity to improve by selecting from several possible strategies. Their competitive mobility is limited, however, by the actions of firms in strong or leading positions.

Tenable competitors exhibit performance that may justify continuation of the business, particularly if there are significant exit barriers. The opportunities to improve position are not obvious, however, as not many plausible strategies are available, and these firms consequently have a less-than-average opportunity to improve themselves. In the early 1980s Burroughs in the computer industry and American Motors in automobiles were tenable competitors.

Tenable competitors sometimes carry on business operations for many years. General Motors may have tolerated AMC in order to price against the costs of the least efficient producer in the industry; AMC's continued existence probably served as well to protect GM against possible antitrust scrutiny.

Weak competitors usually complete the lineup of players in an industry. The unsatisfactory market and financial performance of these businesses reflects significant competitive weakness. They must improve quickly if they are to survive, but in most cases the probability of a turnaround is small. As a result, they ultimately withdraw from the industry.

PORTFOLIO ANALYSIS

Portfolio analysis was a popular tool in strategic planning for at least two decades. However, it has recently fallen into disrepute for being misleading or too simplistic. This is unfortunate because portfolio analysis, applied with discretion and sensitivity, can be a powerful weapon in the practical strategist's armory.

Caveat: Use portfolio analysis primarily to *describe* the current or expected situation rather than to prescribe strategic behavior. A portfolio display, in other words, must be viewed as a device for organizing information in a way that facilitates strategic decisions. It cannot be used to dictate strategy; it can only summarize current conditions and suggest potential future performance.

In the typical contemporary firm, portfolio analysis comprises first a redefinition of organizational units into businesses (SBUs or SBCs). One of the standard classification schemes is then applied to identify the relative strength or competitive position of the business unit and the maturity or attractiveness of its industry and market. Strategy selection and resource allocation then follow.

The portfolio methods in common use include the growth/share matrix, the maturity/competitive position matrix, the attractiveness/strength matrix, and the advantage matrix.

Growth/Share Matrix

Drawing upon the insights provided by the experience curve,[7] the 2×2 matrix devised by the Boston Consulting Group (BCG) in the early 1960s was the progenitor of all subsequent portfolio analysis. The essential premise of this matrix (Figure 3–8) is that higher market share

Figure 3–8.   The Growth/Share Matrix.

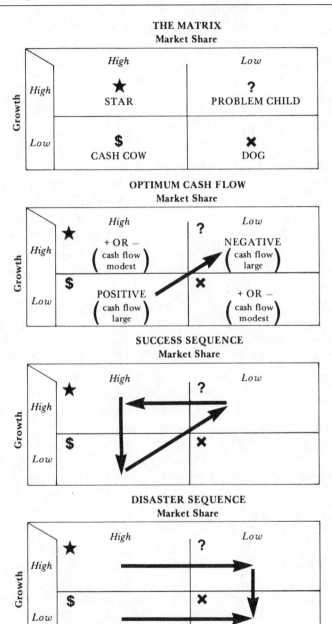

Source: Bruce D. Henderson, *On Corporate Strategy* (Cambridge, Mass.: Abt Books, 1979).
Reprinted with permission.

(greater experience) leads to lower cost. As a result, high-share businesses benefit from an intrinsic competitive advantage that can be utilized to reduce price, putting other high cost competitors at a serious disadvantage. Alternatively, price can be maintained at the historic market level, producing higher profit and cash flow for the competitor with lowest costs. To standardize the application of the BCG methodology across a corporation, the boundary between high and low share (relative to the largest competitor) is often set at 1.5; the boundary between high growth and low growth is usually set at 10 percent.

A corporation's most attractive businesses (the stars) are those with high market share in high growth markets, where sales can be expanded without necessarily taking share from others. Stars exhibit strong and increasing profit and cash flow. Businesses with high market share in slow growth markets (the cash cows) also display good profit and cash flow, but their long-term growth potential is limited. Question mark or problem child businesses have small shares in growing markets— their futures are uncertain. Finally, the businesses having small shares of slow-growth markets are uncharitably denoted as dogs.

The standard success sequence has stars ultimately evolving to cows, question marks successfully managed to become stars, and dogs being eliminated. The net cash outflow from stars and cows is reallocated to fuel the ascension of question marks to stronger positions in the portfolio. In the disaster sequence, stars degenerate to question marks and then to dogs, while cash cows mutate directly to dogs.

Critics of BCG's 2 × 2 matrix invoke a variety of examples to demonstrate that neither high market share or rapid market growth is a prerequisite to succes. For example, Goodyear, the leader in tires with 40 percent market share, realized only a 7 percent return on capital in the five-year period from 1975 to 1979. Maytag, on the other hand, has demonstrated an impressive 27 percent return with only 5 percent of the U.S. appliance market. Competitors in the U.S. airline industry (growing at an annual rate of 13.6 percent) earned a return on capital of only 5.7 percent, whereas competitors in some slow growth industries, such as beverages and tobacco, earned much higher returns. Do these findings invalidate the utility of the 2 × 2 matrix? Hardly.

The reconciliation of these anomalies rests on two key insights. The first key is that market share in these data do not always refer to the *served* market. Thus, although the overall share of Maytag in home appliances is low, its share is high in the niche it serves. This explains why some niche competitors are substantially more profitable than the apparent industry leaders. The corollary to this argument, of course, is that a business can always be able to consider itself as the leader if it defines itself as participating in a small enough market segment. Conversely, the businesss unit that defines the market too broadly ("service," or "transportation") will always report a minuscule market share, even when it is a strong or leading competitor in its served market.

The second insight is that performance is clearly the result of the interaction of more than two variables (share and growth). Market share, after all, is merely a surrogate for competitive position; we can all bring to mind examples of businesses with high share and weak position. The A&P company was the share leader in the 1950s in retail supermarkets. But its small stores in urban locations could not compete effectively with firms that established large stores with broad product lines in up-scale suburbs. U.S. Steel was still the share leader in the 1960s—while it was losing money. Conversely, as we have already implied, low-share competitors may be leaders, as witness Steinway's strong position in pianos with a mere 6 percent market share. Rapidly growing markets, furthermore, are not necessarily attractive, and other variables (including industry structure and investment intensity) influence profitability.

Maturity/Competitive Position Matrix

If 2×2 is good, 4×5 must be better. In this portfolio model, developed at Arthur D. Little (ADL), market share is replaced by competitive position, and market growth becomes industry maturity (Figure 3–9). Although competitive position cannot be computed precisely, it can be assessed with considerable confidence, as pointed out earlier. And although industry maturity is a complex concept, it too can be estimated with some precision.

The multivariate measures of competitive position and industry maturity provide a better measure of strategic condition than the simplistic metrics of the 2×2 matrix, and this matrix offers greater opportunity to differentiate one business from another. In addition, businesses tend to move naturally from one position to another as the industry evolves, so the 4×5 is more helpful than the 2×2 as a tool to develop projections.

As with other portfolio models, however, the 4×5 matrix must be used primarily to describe the condition of a business or set of businesses at a particular time (the position of competitors relative to one another is always in flux), and not as a prescriptive device.

Figure 3–9.   Strategic Position by Competitor.

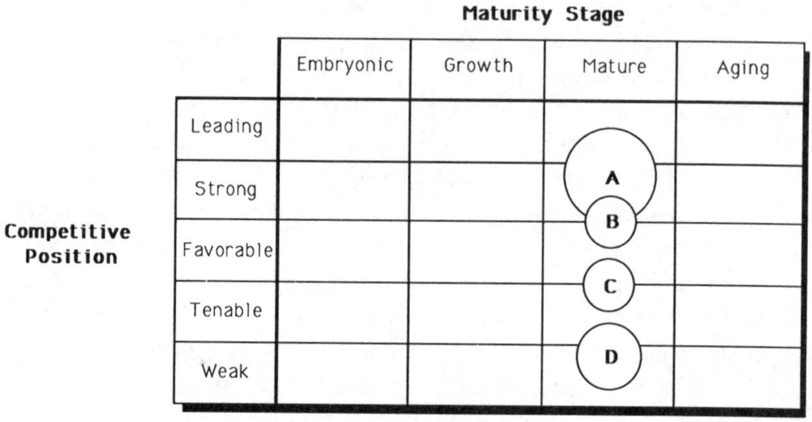

Maturity Stage

		Embryonic	Growth	Mature	Aging
	Leading				
	Strong			A	
Competitive Position	Favorable			B	
	Tenable			C	
	Weak			D	

Attractiveness/Strength Matrix

The strategic disarray at GE in the late 1960s resulted in a collaboration with McKinsey & Company, Inc. that spawned still another portfolio analysis technique. In the GE/McKinsey matrix, the notion of market share or competitive position is replaced by business strength, while market growth or industry maturity becomes industry attractiveness (Figure 3–10).

Analyzing business strength means attempting to summarize the ability of the business unit to succeed in the industry. In this sense business strength is synonymous with competitive position. Customary components of business strength are market share, share growth, quality, technology, cost, marketing, and relative profitability.

Assessing industry attractiveness is subjective. For this reason the nine-box matrix (3×3) should be used primarily at the corporate level (what is attractive to the managers of the business may be unattractive to the managers of the corporation). It follows similarly that an industry that is attractive to one corporation may be shunned by another. A corporation that is cash rich may feel most comfortable with a capital-intensive industry, while a cash-poor corporation may view a nonintensive service industry as more attractive. Firms that participate

Figure 3–10. GE/McKinsey Strength/Attractiveness Matrix.

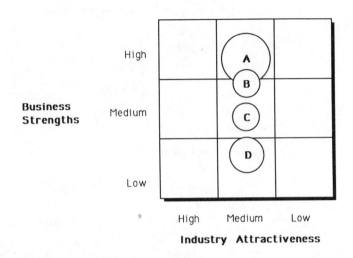

Source: Adapted with permission from McKinsey & Company, Inc., based on "The McKinsey Nine Box Matrix."

in regulated industries may view unregulated markets as offering greater future growth, while firms in unregulated industries may see regulated industries as a haven from foreign competition.

Advantage Matrix

A more recent version of the 2×2 matrix focuses attention on the importance of competitive advantage. The classification scheme (Figure 3–11) suggests that industries fall into four categories as a function of the number of possible competitive advantages and the magnitude of the advantage. For industries in which economies of scale are important, that is, the supply curve has a steep slope, *volume* represents the primary strategic objective. Construction equipment, semiconductors, commercial aircraft, and agricultural equipment fall into this category. The leaders in these industries (Caterpillar, Texas Instruments, Boeing, and Deere) derive competitive advantage from their strong market share.

When economies of scale are unimportant or when they cannot be attained by a particular firm, competitors attempt to differentiate themselves in other ways. If they succeed in gaining significant competitive

Figure 3–11. The Advantage Matrix.

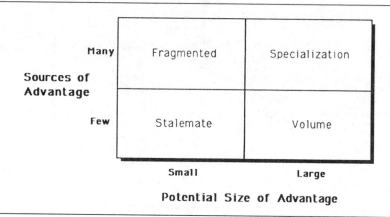

advantage, the industry may fall into the *specialist* category. The calculator, computer, and copier industries contain firms who have differentiated themselves with unique products or features, as witness Hewlett-Packard in calculators, Digital Equipment in minicomputers, and Canon in office copiers.

If neither cost advantage or noncost differentiation is possible, the industry is *stalemated* as exemplified by commodity paper, tires, and cement. In these industries, all competitors share approximately the same cost structure, yet have thus far been unable to differentiate themselves otherwise from one another.

In the final category we find *fragmented* industries in which some small degree of differentiation is possible but the resultant benefits are small. Many distribution businesses fall in this cell, as do foundries, sawmills, print shops, advertising agencies, and most retailers.

Recreational boats is a good example of a fragmented industry. In 1985 more than 3,000 manufacturers competed for total sales of just over 700,000 units. Although the boating industry overall has grown at 5–10 percent in recent years, in the powerboat category, even Chris-Craft, Bayliner Marine, Sea Ray, and Wellcraft, the best known powerboat companies, each have less than 2 percent of their segment.[8]

Occasionally, firms in fragmented industries find a way to change the rules. White Castle, an important early player in the fast food industry, held to a classic fragmented industry strategy by maintaining small size, narrow product line, and minimum inventory. McDonald's, by its strategy of accelerated growth to achieve major economies of scale in marketing and sourcing, was able to break the rules and move into the volume category. Similarly successful strategies of expansion in fragmented markets have been carried out by Midas (automobile mufflers), Hertz (rental cars) and Century 21 (real estate).

Market share plays a different role in each cell of the advantage matrix. For competitors in the fragmented category, size or market share is not important. Nor is share important in the stalemated category, where no one is highly profitable, regardless of market share. Market share makes the most difference in the volume category, where economies of scale yield low cost and significant entry barriers in many industries.

SUMMARY

Careful analysis of the situation is the practical strategist's prelude to strategy formulation, for it is the externalities of industry, market, and competition that determine the strategy possibilities. The manager who launches a strategy based only on the strengths and weaknesses of his own firm takes high risks. A business is strong or weak only relative to competitors.

The structure of most industries evolves dramatically over time. Thus, as a prelude to strategy formulation, managers must develop not only a picture of the industry today but also a scenario for an appropriate future time horizon. The horizon may be only a few years for volatile industries such as toys, software, or fashion but may need to be many years for forest products, electric utilities, or distilled spirits, for example. Industries that are benignly competitive today may develop vicious rivalries as markets mature, new technology is introduced, or the basis of competition changes.

Examining the details of industry structure yields insight into potential industry profitability. Understanding the maturity of the industry suggests likely future changes in structure and performance. Segmenting the market unveils opportunities to develop or enhance competitive advantage (implying in fact that the strategy of the business is preordained by the choice of market segments to be served). And understanding the behavior of competitors reveals their strategies, their commitment to the industry, ultimately allowing the business analyst to establish a long-term scenario for a business's own success.

Careful situation analysis is a prelude to strategy selection, for it helps identify the range of strategic options. But as industries evolve along their life cycle, their structure changes, and new ways of competing emerge. The practical strategist understands that strategy must change—and gets ready to adapt.

NOTES

1. Michael E. Porter, *Competitive Advantage* (New York: Free Press, 1980) has addressed this subject at length.
2. David Tuller, "What's New in the Tennis Business," *The New York Times*, June 7, 1987, p. 11.
3. Although the demand is less intense than in 1848, when the New England whaling fleet numbered 600 ships, the Naval Company, Inc. still has a profitable business selling harpoons to the Eskimos. Buggy whip demand has never returned to the 1893 peak of over 20 million units, but the Westfield Whip Company dominates the harness racing market, with an estimated 70 percent share, according to Jack Willoughby, "The Last Iceman," *Forbes*, July 13, 1987, p. 187.
4. Alvin Toffler, *Future Shock* (New York: McGraw-Hill, 1985) and John Naisbitt, *Megatrends* (New York: Warner Books, 1982).
5. Dean Silverman, "Field Analysis," *Planning Review* (September 1984).
6. Oreos have been the world's best selling cookie almost since their introduction in 1912. Over 6 billion units were sold in 1985 (a 10 percent share), increasing cumulative sales to over 100 billion units.
7. Based on empirical observation in many industries, the experience curve is the decline of cost and price at a rate proportional to the cumulative industry production (experience).
8. Sailboats represent only 6 percent of the boating industry, and their sales have been declining (except for sailboards, which have been growing 15–20 percent annually).

4 FORMULATING BUSINESS STRATEGY

Every business has a strategy. The strategy may be intentional or unintentional, explicit or implicit, effective or ineffective, but it can always be identified. How can we recognize the strategy of a business? Most reliably by simply observing how the management spends its time, energy, and money. Strategy, in other words, is not necessarily reflected by what business managers say. What they *do* is more revealing.

A business can select from many possible strategies, but most strategies will not work. Even enthusiasm cannot overcome the handicap of bad strategy, as witness the debacle of the Light Brigade.[1] And a good—even brilliant—strategy today may be a losing strategy tomorrow, as Friden, the dominant force in the mechanical calculator industry, and RCA, the early leader in color television, have shown us. Conversely, as we have observed, good strategies do not yield good results unless they are implemented well.

Competitors rarely go head to head, because ingenious sidestepping brings higher returns. Burning down the competitor's factory is illegal, and bringing legal action against the competitor only works if he is acting illegally! Thus, competition is nearly always indirect: We seek to deprive the competitor of revenue by making our products and services more attractive to his customers or by making it unprofitable for the competitor to provide similar products and services. Competitive success can also derive from dealing more effectively than competitors

61

with suppliers or distributors—that is, by interdicting the competitor's value chain. But whatever we do (in other words, whatever our strategy), our effectiveness must be gauged primarily in terms of performance or position relative to our competitors.

A more precise definition of business strategy for our purpose:

Business strategy is the way resources are allocated to improve or maintain competitive advantage.

Thus, improving market share or profitability is not a strategy, but rather the result of a strategy.

In many businesses, strategy is implicit. Managers may not have enunciated explicit allocation guidelines in advance of the actual commitment of resources. For that matter, unfortunately for novices, strategy selection is not a simple linear process, and the process by which experienced managers select strategy for a business is an art form that is difficult to describe. Like chess masters, they recognize immediately the small set of strategies that are likely to work in a particular situation and ignore all the other theoretical alternatives. The amateur (or new MBA) must search through a larger set of possibilities, while attempting to answer the following questions:

- What strategies are available in principle?
- Which ones will work (what are the feasible alternatives)?
- What will they cost to implement?
- What results can be expected from each?
- How will the competitors respond?

And ultimately,

- What strategy makes the most sense?

Strategy selection is often biased by a set of predetermined objectives, in which case the feasible alternatives must be matched (perhaps awkwardly) to the objectives. In addition, objectives are often unrealistic, having been arbitrarily imposed by corporate management.[2] Managers in most organizations respond with a correspondingly arbitrary set of strategies.

The best and most creative strategies emerge when managers are given the opportunity to select strategy in the absence of any external constraints; their recommendations can be tempered later by corporate needs. Thus, the practical strategist does not attempt to find a strategy that meets certain arbitrary objectives—that is, fills the gap. Instead, objectives are established *after* the most appropriate strategies are selected.

As the practical strategist will recognize, any apparent dichotomy between strategies (the means) and results (the ends) is artificial, for strategies and results cannot be separated. (The Möbius strip—a topological loop having only one surface—is a good metaphor for this connectivity and inseparability.) Strategy is the way (the means) that a manager achieves desirable business results (the ends). Thus, it is futile to set objectives and goals that cannot be attained by any plausible strategy, unless some minimal level of performance is necessary to assure survival. (Nor should managers select strategy capriciously.) However, realistically projecting the results or outcome of a proposed strategy allows a manager to determine whether that strategy will allow the business to meet its stated objectives. The practical strategist, in other words, assesses the acceptability of the results expected from a particular strategy. The "results" can then be elevated to the status of "objectives" or "goals."

STRATEGY SELECTION, STEP BY STEP

The first step in selecting business strategy (and sometimes also the last step) is to hypothesize a strategy vector, a direction of movement relative to competitors. Three possibilities are available:

Improve competitive position.   This is the vector of choice for most growth-oriented North American managers. It is also a natural choice for businesses in the early stages of an industry life cycle. Later in the life cycle, on the other hand, attempting to improve competitive position is likely to be unattractive (the cost will exceed the benefit) or impossible (stronger competitors may prove to be invulnerable).

Maintain competitive position.   This vector is the natural choice for most businesses in mature industries. It by no means implies passivity; substantial investment and a long-term commitment may be required simply to defend a position against aggressive competitors. The average business runs hard just to stay in place, as witness the massive expenditures made by Ford (to keep up with GM and the Japanese), DEC (to keep pace with IBM), Pepsi (to run with Coca-Cola), and Burger King (to maintain share versus McDonald's).

Withdraw or harvest.   Withdrawal from the market is the most sensible strategic choice if a business is weak relative to competitors and unlikely to improve its position within a reasonable time. When properly managed (assuming the decision is made explicitly), this strategy may yield very high return to the stockholders.[3] General Electric's sale of its computer business to Honeywell and American Can's withdrawal from packaging are two examples of successful withdrawal.

The strategy for a business, regardless of the vector selected, entails two decisions:

1. Which market will my business serve?

Almost every business will find that serving a particular segment or segments is more attractive than attempting to serve the entire market, unless overall market share is sought to achieve advantages of scale. The attractive segment may or may not be one that is growing rapidly, but it must offer the business a potential competitive advantage.

Frank Perdue, as an example, has succeeded in the broiler chicken industry (attaining 50 percent market share) by concentrating resources on the $800 million New England market. Piedmont Air flourished after airline deregulation by serving midsized cities ignored by the larger airlines; despite higher fares, it grew to one of the nation's largest carriers. Zenith Data Systems established a position in the computer industry by concentrating on supplying business and government markets, beating out IBM for a recent Internal Revenue Service contract.

As these examples suggest, the most attractive market segment is not always the one that is exciting or glamorous; it is the one in which you have an opportunity to excel. It is the segment in which your firm's competitive strengths are greater than those of your competitors.

2. How can I achieve advantage in this market?

In the final analysis, competitive advantage can only be the result of *differentiation* from competition in a way that adds value to the customer group. This differentiation may be achieved by either low cost or by offering unique features, functions or performance to customers, in other words by differentiating the product or the process.[4] Those who are unable to differentiate in a way that customers value will incur a competitive disadvantage. If sustained over a long period of time, this disadvantage will lead to failure.

Achieving competitive advantage by differentiation through *low cost* was the strategy of choice for many businesses in the 1960s and 1970s. Low cost may be the result of access to cheap resources (raw materials, labor, or capital), but it may also derive from efficiencies in the production process. As a result, following the logic of the theory of the experience curve, firms sought to achieve high market share in order to realize the lower cost associated with greater throughput. A low-cost competitor could either reduce price to place opponents at a competitive disadvantage, or maintain price to realize higher margins and cash flow. In the second instance, competitors run the risk of supporting a price umbrella that allows marginal competitors to continue or new competitors to enter the game.

Low cost is not important in some industries, especially in the early stages of their evolution (hand calculators, personal computers) or when image and reputation are important selling features (cosmetics, men's and women's fashions). Low-share competitors, furthermore, may not be able to achieve cost leadership no matter what they do, particularly if the industry offers the opportunity for significant economies of scale. In these situations, competitors must attempt to differentiate themselves in other ways.

Differentiation on a *noncost* basis entails finding a way to provide higher value to customers, such as product features, service, distribution, reliability, or image. This may allow higher prices and margins to be realized. If an improved product offering results in greater unit sales, costs may also decline, demonstrating that cost and noncost strategies are often interdependent. Some firms (Caterpillar in materials handling, Philip Morris in cigarettes) have successfully invoked both methods of differentiation. Usually, however, the choices are mutually exclusive, as witness Whirlpool versus Maytag (home appliances) and Goodyear versus Michelin (tires).[5]

DIFFERENTIATION:
THE AUTOMOTIVE INDUSTRY

After the introduction of the high-speed internal combustion engine by Daimler in 1885, the market grew slowly. But in the early 1900s, Henry Ford established a low-cost standardized automobile design that allowed interchange of motor and chassis among different models. In 1913 he introduced a complete assembly line for the Model T (available in any color as long as it was black, the fastest drying color), and cost fell rapidly. Ford slashed prices from $950 to less than $300, and annual output rose from 5,986 units in 1908 to over 800,000 ten years later. Ford's market share vaulted from 9 percent in 1909 to 55 percent in 1921, the result of successful differentiation on the basis of both price and cost.

In the early 1920s General Motors adopted an alternative differentiation strategy when it introduced style and color for $100 more than Ford's car (low price was no longer the name of the game). GM segmented the market and changed the basis of competition, and by 1926 Ford's share had dropped to 33 percent. Ford closed operations in 1926 to design and produce the new Model A. But the Ford strategy in 1927 did not change; it again combined low price, standardized design, and mass production. GM's competitive position continued to improve, and only in the mid-1980s has Ford recovered any of its lost share.

The number of competitors in the automobile industry subsequently declined as well. In 1929 the industry comprised 108 competitors. By 1940 the number had dwindled to 44, and by 1950 only 5 players remained. The early leaders in automobile manufacture such as Reo, Essex, Hudson, Studebaker, Auburn, Cord, Winton, and Packard were either merged or acquired.

THE LAWS OF STRATEGY

The methods, principles, and models that relate to strategy formulation are numerous. Some work most effectively in conjunction with others. Others succeed only in specific situations. Novice strategists are often confused by the profusion of alternatives and react by selecting an unrealistically large, difficult, or incongruent set of strategies. This is the normal result of the first of my two laws:

Allio's First Law: Many strategies exist.

The practical strategist, however, also understands the significance of my second law:

Allio's Second Law: Few strategies work.

Most strategies fail because they ignore the basis of competition in the industry, or because they lack the resources to be implemented successfully, or because they fail to foresee the competitive reaction. The essence of effective strategy formulation, and the difference between "enlightened" and "typical" strategies, lies in the selection of those few that will allow the manager to outperform his competitors, to establish and maintain a competitive advantage.

In an emerging industry, for example, the creative manager can devise numerous ways to differentiate the product or service from the

Figure 4–1. Realistic Strategic Options Over the Life Cycle.

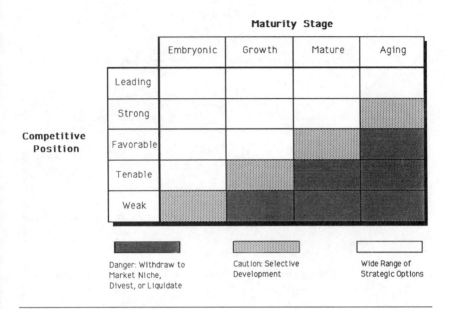

competition, while still providing value to the customer. On the other hand, the weak player in a dying industry may find that he has only one strategy left: to get out. This suggests the intuitively agreeable notion of a finite set of *natural* strategies—strategies that actually make sense for a particular competitor.

The set of natural strategies is largest for the leading or strong competitor in the early stages of an industry's evolution. As competitive position deteriorates, the natural set becomes smaller. As an industry matures, the realistic strategic options also become fewer, particularly if competitive position is simultaneously declining, as illustrated in Figure 4–1. In superconductivity (an emerging technology), for example, many strategy options are available, and even weak competitors have a chance to play. In a mature industry such as textiles, however, only the strongest competitors have any real strategic latitude. The leader in any industry has virtually unlimited choice of strategy (even though some may be manifestly better than others).

Since the basis of competition in an industry (the key success factors) changes as the industry matures, the strategic emphasis of the successful competitor also changes, as illustrated in Figure 4–2. In the early stages of an industry, expansion by marketing and product innovation are

Figure 4–2. Strategic Emphasis by Industry Stage.

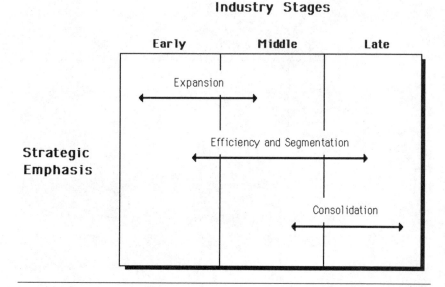

important. In the mature stages of an industry, segmenting the market, adding value, and improving efficiency emerge as key strategy elements. And in the late stages of an industry, consolidation and rationalization become the touchstones for success. A natural strategy in one stage of an industry's evolution may be a prescription for disaster in another. Consider the following examples:

Backward integration is adopted by a business to secure a source of supply or add value to the total production process. This strategy may be perfectly appropriate in the mature, stable stage of an industry. But it is extremely risky in embryonic industries when technologies and customers' needs are changing rapidly. Nor does it often make sense in a declining industry, when new investment will yield low returns relative to other opportunities. An exception occurs when a source of raw material needs to be secured by acquiring a stake in a key supplier.

Price reduction is adopted by a business in order to secure a larger share of the market or to maintain share. This strategy is irrelevant in the early stages of an industry, when the bases of competition are usually product features, product function, or sometimes mere product availability. Nor does it make sense in the later stages of an industry, when price reductions will usually be matched quickly by competitors. But in the growth stage, price reduction can increase share, particularly if a competitor is the low-cost manufacturer or if other firms lack the resources to match price.[6] It is also effective when lower price provides access to new markets, as witnessed by Du Pont's strategy for nylon or the strategy adopted by most competitors in the personal computer industry.

New product development is adopted to maintain or expand revenues in existing markets. This strategy is most natural in the embryonic and growth stages of an industry as competitors strive to secure market position. But as the industry matures, process development begins to replace product development as the strategy of choice. Why? Because the basis of competition has shifted in most industries to include price. Price competition demands low cost as a prerequisite to survival, and low cost generally is the consequence of improvements in process technology.

The idea of natural strategy does not mean that innovation in mature industries is to be discouraged. Line extension strategies, for example, can be very effective. Long-term winners in the $12 billion toy industry have included Mattell (250 million Barbie-family dolls sold since Barbie's debut in 1959), Interlego A/S (the Danish multinational that sells Lego bricks in 125 countries[7]), and Hasbro (GI Joe and Jem—Barbie's new competitor). 3M, to cite another example, has demanded for years that all its businesses renew themselves by generating 25 percent of their revenues from products developed within the past five years. But the task of developing new products becomes increasingly difficult as firms become larger, and the number of new products needed to maintain growth will increase exponentially. It is not surprising, then, to observe some managers seeking growth by acquisition.

A summary of guidelines to natural strategies for industries at different stages in the life cycle is given by Figure 4–3. We need to reiterate, however, that the competitive position of a business will also influence its choice of strategy.

The dominant competitor in any industry, regardless of its maturity, can by definition play the game in any way it wants, constrained only by the needs of its consumers or suppliers (or regulatory agencies). Dominant competitors also experience high profitability, as witness the sterling records of IBM, Du Pont, and Procter & Gamble in certain businesses. Similar performance can be found when competitors band together to form cartels (diamonds, oil, and copper).

Figure 4–3. Natural Strategy Execution.

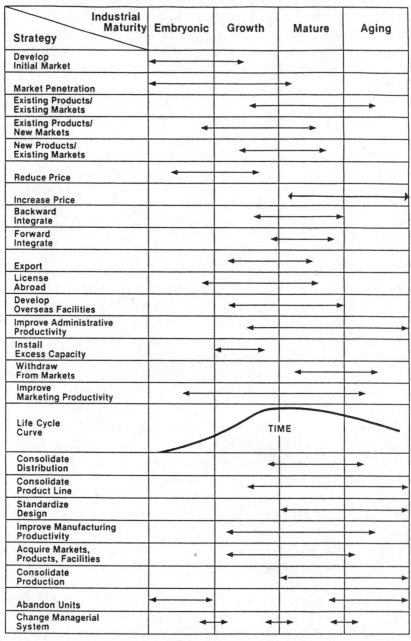

Industrial Maturity / Strategy	Embryonic	Growth	Mature	Aging
Develop Initial Market	←	→		
Market Penetration	←		→	
Existing Products/ Existing Markets		←		→
Existing Products/ New Markets		←	→	
New Products/ Existing Markets		←	→	
Reduce Price	←	→		
Increase Price			←	→
Backward Integrate		←	→	
Forward Integrate		←	→	
Export		←	→	
License Abroad		←	→	
Develop Overseas Facilities		←	→	
Improve Administrative Productivity		←		→
Install Excess Capacity		←	→	
Withdraw From Markets			←	→
Improve Marketing Productivity	←			→
Life Cycle Curve			TIME	
Consolidate Distribution			←	→
Consolidate Product Line		←		→
Standardize Design			←	→
Improve Manufacturing Productivity		←		→
Acquire Markets, Products, Facilities		←		→
Consolidate Production			←	→
Abandon Units	←	→	←	→
Change Managerial System	←→	←→	←→	

←——→ Span of Arrow Indicates Appropriate Timeframe to Implement Given Strategy

Figure 4–4. Typical Strategy Options by Competitive Position.

	LEADER	FOLLOWER
MARKET	Dominate	Find a Niche
PRODUCT	Offer Broad Line	Specialize
TECHNOLOGY	Innovate	Imitate
VALUE ADDED	Integrate	Subcontract
MANUFACTURING	Automate	Emphasize Flexibility

As suggested in Figure 4–4, leaders in general act to maintain or improve competition by improving quality, introducing new products, and intensifying marketing expenditures. At the same time, they usually have the resources to invest in vertical integration or productivity improvement, strategies that enhance profitability.

The strategy adopted by 3M to preserve its position in Post-it note pads is classic leadership strategy: improve brand recognition, fill all the niches (color, form, size, printed and unprinted), add ancillary products (dispensers), and saturate the distribution channels, thus making it difficult for any new competitor to enter this lucrative market. Leaders cover all the bets.

The greatest strategic challenge is probably faced by businesses having a favorable competitive position in a mature industry (cell C3 in the ADL matrix). To begin with, this is probably the most congested cell in the matrix; the majority of U.S. businesses can be found in this position. By definition firms in this cell constantly face stronger competitors above them. As a result the successful strategy requires a great deal of sensitivity and selectivity. Some common approaches to improving position from this situation (not all are recommended) include the following:

Hurl resources at the opposition.   The rewards of this common strategy in many consumer goods industries rarely justify the investment. Strong players usually retaliate in kind, so no one wins, and a stalemate often ensues.

Acquire a competitor.   This is a less expensive strategy, although acquiring a strong player often requires payment of a substantial premium. Recent examples of this strategy include the North American Philips' acquisition of Westinghouse's lighting business and the proposed purchase of AMC by Chrysler.

Wait for a blunder.   Waiting requires great patience, although it may pay off handsomely in the short run (Johnson & Johnson's competitors after the Tylenol debacle) or in the long run (share gains by Miller and Anheuser-Busch after Schlitz's reformulation of its leading brand).

Segment the market.   This is the rational approach to gaining share. It explains how even weak competitors can gain position against giants like Kodak, Western Electric, IBM, and Xerox who become lazy or lose vigilance. The usurpation of the minicomputer market segment by DEC and the personal computer market segment by Apple exemplify this strategy.

Savin's office copier strategy in the late 1970s offers a grand example of segmentation strategy. Although Xerox held as much as 80 percent of the U.S. plain paper copier market, Savin and its Japanese partner Ricoh were able to offer a low priced plain paper copier that soon achieved 40 percent share in this neglected niche while generating handsome returns on equity. The Xerox share of the overall market plummeted as customers turned to new sources to satisfy their needs for distributed copying.

Weak businesses may have many strategic choices in the beginning when there is no leader but find their options closed out quickly as the industry matures. They often attempt to improve their lot by emulating the strategies of the industry leaders, but this usually hastens their demise. Thinking about the importance of meeting the basis of competition quickly highlights why this occurs. For example, the backward integration available to a strong competitor is exceedingly risky for a weak competitor who has limited resources, thin margins, and little flexibility; the firm's high fixed costs make it extremely vulnerable to downturns in market demand.

Strategies such as price reduction, new product development, and increased advertising or promotion are further examples of imprudent strategies for a weak competitor. The attempt of Chrysler in the 1960s to emulate GM's broad product line was an example of such imprudence. AMC's announced intent in 1987 to offer a new line of luxury automobiles represents similar misguided judgment, unless Renault (the parent) is prepared to spend heavily to secure a narrow foothold in the U.S. market.

Merger with other firms in the industry is an obvious consideration for weak competitors. Little is usually gained, however, by merging with another weak player, as demonstrated by the recent alliance between Burroughs and Sperry (a marginal competitor) to form Unisys. American Motors more plausibly has attempted to stem its decline by forming strategic alliances with various European automobile manufacturers, such as Renault, and with U.S. manufacturers, such as Chrysler.

The low-share competitor's task must be to build share while minimizing competitive vulnerability. In fact, as an industry matures and consolidates, a competitor must improve absolute share simply to maintain parity. And cash traps (funds invested that can never be recovered) abound, for the business must finance inflation and industry growth, as well as growth in market share. Practical strategies for the small competitor include the following:

- Sell products that are critical to the customer.
- Focus on regional markets.
- Concentrate on segments where service is important.
- Sell to captive markets.
- Avoid high investment.
- Emphasize product quality.
- Keep marketing expenses low.
- Avoid situations where suppliers are integrated forward.

The most creative strategies for small businesses entail redefining the market. The secret to success is often to focus on segments in which small scale is not a handicap. This may mean reduced scope (for example, the strategies of Crown Cork & Seal in containers and Jensen in loudspeakers), new segments or innovative products (for example, Miller in light beer, Honda in motorcycles, Bic in disposable pens, Savin and Canon in copiers, Cray in supercomputers), or new channels of distribution (for example, Hanes in pantyhose).

Domino's has achieved a strong position in the $8 billion pizza industry by focusing on the $2 billion delivery segment. By promising delivery within 30 minutes, Domino's share of delivered pizzas has approached 50 percent nationally. And Snap-on Tools Corporation has achieved a consistent 21 percent return on equity by charging more for the benefit of its premium quality tools delivered through "wagon-jobbers" at regular intervals to the customers.

FUNCTIONAL STRATEGIES

Note that while any strategy may emphasize a particular functional dimension, such as marketing or production, business strategies in general require contributions from several functions in the organization; that is, they cut across functional boundaries. Many planning processes fail to recognize these interdependencies, as managers learn when they try to implement their newly developed strategic plans. Put another way, functional strategies (activities carried out exclusively in a certain function such as marketing or production) are almost always part of a more comprehensive business strategy.

In all cases the selection of a functional strategy must be driven by the overall strategy for the business. Otherwise, the resulting lack of goal congruence leads to failure to implement either functional or business strategy. Technology strategies, as one example, fall into three classes, grouped by the purpose of the technology effort:

Product Technology.   Technological resources are allocated to develop new products, to improve product quality or value, or to extend the product line by making the product perform faster or longer. The success of Procter & Gamble with Tide detergent is exemplary. Since its introduction in 1947, the product has been modified 55 times without changing its basic function or its target market.

But in many industries, standardization or incremental innovation overtakes the manager's inclination toward dramatic technological innovation. At the turn of the century, for example, consumers of automobiles had access to an impressive array of alternatives. The market included cars powered by steam, electricity, and gas, open or closed cars having three or four wheels, and a variety of structural and performance options.[8] By 1987, however, technological diversity had virtually disappeared, and consumer options were limited to relatively modest variations in style or performance.

Process Technology.   During the late growth stage of the life cycle, price competition arises. As a result, low cost becomes a key success factor, and the focus of technological advance shifts to improving process. Improvement takes the form of equipment redesign to improve yield or throughput, change in process (for example, from forging to die casting), or automation in the factory or office. Material substitutions are often an outgrowth of this strategy.

Basic Research.   Technological leaders direct significant resources to the search for breakthroughs in existing technologies and the discovery of new technologies. Being a leader in technology is not, however, a prerequisite to success. A number of industry leaders, including many U.S., Japanese, and Korean firms, have flourished by committing to a strategy of being a technological follower. It was, after all, Sperry Rand, not IBM, who brought the first commercial computer to the marketplace.

Indeed, technological leadership may require the expenditure of resources that are beyond the means of most firms. For many firms, adopting new technology shortly after its application by others may be just as good as being first. And conversely, holding on to old technology too long may be fatal. Curtiss Wright was number 28 on the Fortune 500 list in 1945. But Curtiss Wright bet on piston engines too long, and Boeing took the lead in aircraft manufacture.

Businesses blessed with strong competitive positions should consider assuming technological leadership; those who are weak should follow the leader (quickly, if possible). And the resource allocation focus should shift in any case from product innovation to process innovation as the industry matures.

STRATEGY MAPS

Mapping competitors' strategies is often a helpful precursor to selecting strategy. Competitors can often be assigned to strategy groups, based on the market segments they serve. In theory, competitors' strategies will be appropriate only for the markets served by their own strategy group, and mobility barriers will prohibit competitors from penetrating the other segments.

Figure 4–5 presents a strategy map for the U.S. gas-powered chain saw industry in 1976. In the professional group, typified by Stihl, we find a group of firms committed to serving professional users with high-quality products sold through a network of dealers able to provide service. Firms such as McCulloch (Black & Decker) in the branded mass market group distribute average quality chain saws to the casual user through mass merchandisers. And firms such as Beaird-Poulan focus on the sales of lower quality products under private label. Skil had adopted a unique niche strategy, marketing high-quality products almost exclusively to the construction industry.

Figure 4–5. Strategy Map of the U.S. Chain Saw Industry.

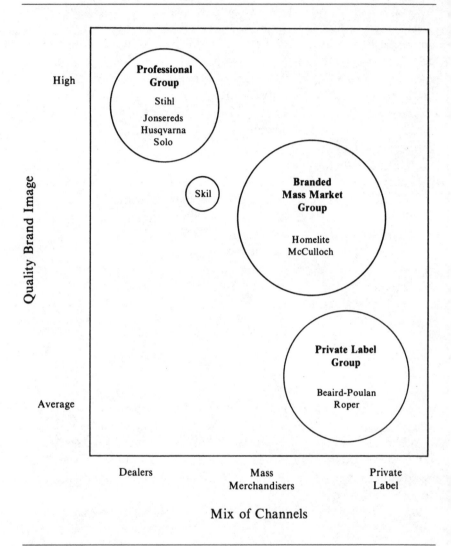

Mix of Channels

Any firm, of course, may elect to serve many markets or become a specialist. When a niche strategy is chosen, the niche must be defensible against strong competitors having broad product lines; that is, entry barriers to the niche must be high. In chain saws, therefore, it is hard for Stihl to serve the mass market of casual users, because Stihl lacks distribution. Nor could Black & Decker effectively serve the professional users, because it cannot provide service.

Other industries with clearly distinguishable strategy groups have included hand-held calculators, plastics, and home appliances. Calculator manufacturers fall into two distinct groups: technological leaders marketing complex, high-quality products to sophisticated buyers (for example, Hewlett-Packard) and low-cost producers marketing simpler products to the mass market (for example, Texas Instruments). Plastics manufacturers are distinguished by degree of vertical integration: oil companies such as Amoco (highly integrated) versus chemical companies such as Hoechst (specialized products, lower vertical integration). The home appliance industry can be mapped using a combination of product and market categories. Maytag sells high-quality products to image- or brand-conscious consumers; Whirlpool focuses on moderate quality, midpriced products for mass markets; while General Electric has historically sought the low-end home contractor market.

EMPIRICISM IN STRATEGY FORMULATION

Classic approaches to strategy formulation were based largely on the premise that every business is unique. Managers believed that insights into strategy for the future could be derived from historical extrapolation (what worked last year might work again). Some "sophisticated" firms even examined what the competition was doing.

The approach taken by most business schools in teaching strategy reinforced this practice. They subjected students to a barrage of cases hoping that students would develop skills in processing large amounts of data and learn to distinguish important information from irrelevant facts. This philosophy required the construction of an extensive anecdotal data base that would prepare future managers for new situations they might encounter.

The need for common sense and intuition has not abated. Rather it is reinforced every time we see other firms embark on strategies that we are sure will be unsuccessful. The number of strategy variables alone is overwhelmingly large, and it takes considerable experience to know how to use them most effectively.

Even experienced strategists, however, recognize the benefits to be derived from codifying the vast array of strategy choices, and from applying quantitative tools that can help a manager narrow the array of logical choices to those satisfying my Second Law—the few strategies that work!

Significant progress was made possible when the Profit Impact of Market Strategy (PIMS) program[9] introduced and legitimized the use of empiricism in strategy formulation. The singular contribution of this research program has been to invoke the possibility that laws of business exist in the same way that laws of natural science ($F = ma$; $E = mc^2$) have been identified. In particular, PIMS research has confirmed that a business unit's performance correlates directly with strategic decisions. Indeed, despite criticism of the statistical methods used to build the PIMS model (for example, the allegation that multicollinearity perturbs the results), the model explains as much as 60–70 percent of the profit performance (return on investment) of a business. The balance is attributed to the skill of individual managers and to residuals that cannot be explained by the model.

According to PIMS analysis, the major strategic determinants of business profitability (relative to competitors) are the following:

- Quality
- Market share
- Capacity utilization
- Investment intensity
- Direct cost
- Fixed capital intensity
- Market/sales
- New products (percentage of total sales)

The mathematical form of the relationships between strategy and performance is complex, of course, and must be expressed in the form of a multivariate regression equation.

The explanatory power of the PIMS model rests largely on cross-sectional analysis, the pooling of data from businesses in many different industries. The critical hypothesis is thus that the specific characteristics of an industry are less important in determining performance than strategic attributes shared by businesses in many industries. This finding has given rise to the powerful notion of *strategy peers*.[10] A strategy peer is defined as a business in one industry having a strategic condition (for example, relative market share, investment intensity, product quality) similar to a business in another industry. Thus, in the early 1980s, the U.S. leader in automobiles (GM) might have compared itself with similarly positioned firms in farm equipment (Deere) or airlines (United).

A weak firm like Chrysler would select Massey-Ferguson and Pan Am or Braniff as strategy peers.

Although the findings of the PIMS program have been widely publicized, few managers have chosen to use the model in practicing strategy formulation. This may be explained in part by the complexity and highly quantitative nature of the model—its black box quality. Thus, when results from the model are intuitively agreeable (for example, high market share produces high profit) the utility of the model is impugned ("We knew that already"). When the results are counterintuitive, however, the validity of the model is questioned ("The model is wrong," managers say).

OTHER STRATEGY MODELS

Business strategy has deep roots in the principles of military strategy explicated as early as the sixth century B.C. by Chinese philosopher Sun Tzu in *The Art of War* and later in 1832 by Karl von Clausewitz in his *On War.* More recently Liddell Hart has set down in *Strategy* (1967) a number of military axioms that apply to business. He observes that concentration of strength against weakness is a key guideline; dislocation of the enemy's psychological and physical balance is often a prelude to his overthrow. To ensure reaching an objective, Hart emphasizes the importance of alternatives and cautions the strategist not to attack while the opponent is on guard.

Trout and Ries suggest that firms in the competitive arena have four strategic options:[11]

- *Defensive warfare*
  Only the market leader should consider playing defense.
  The best defensive strategy is the courage to attack yourself.
  Strong competitive moves should always be blocked.
- *Offensive warfare*
  The main consideration is the strength of the leader.
  Attack a weakness in the leader's strength.
  Launch the attack on a narrow front.
- *Flanking warfare*
  Good flanking moves must be made into uncontested area.
  Tactical surprise is important.
  Pursuit is as critical as the attack itself.

- *Guerilla warfare*
  Find a segment small enough to defend.
  Never act like a leader, no matter how successful.
  Be prepared to bug out at a moment's notice.

Unfortunately, the simplicity and generality of this model makes it difficult for many managers to apply.

IMPROVING FINANCIAL PERFORMANCE

As discussed earlier, variance in industry performance can often be explained on the basis of industry structure and maturity. However profitable the industry as a whole, a more important question for most managers is how to improve financial performance within their own segment of the industry—how to beat the averages. Profitability within industries varies considerably more than profitability between industries. That is, even in unattractive industries certain businesses perform exceptionally well. The mean before-tax ROI for a broad spectrum of businesses from the PIMS data base is approximately 20 percent, but some businesses are extremely profitable, while others lose money.

Why are some businesses more profitable than others? It is the combination of strategy and implementation relative to competitors that makes the difference. From a purely accounting point of view, this means having higher margins or better utilization of assets than competitors (turnover of plant and equipment, inventory, and receivables).

Return on net assets (RONA) =   Margin (M) × Turnover (T).

[Net income/Net assets   = Net income/Sales × Sales/Net assets.]

Readers will recognize this as the Du Pont formula, an accounting explanation of profitability. But from a strategic point of view, margins are higher than competitors' margins only if price is higher or cost is lower. These in turn depend on having better quality, higher market share, or greater productivity—all attributes that are driven by business strategy decisions.

Consider the performance of well-managed pharmaceutical firms and well-managed retail druggists. They earn approximately equivalent returns on equity (as shown in Table 4–1) but use dramatically different strategies. Pharmaceutical manufacturers introduce unique, often patent-protected products that can be sold at high prices to a small segment

Table 4–1. Relative Profitability of Producers and
Distributors in the Drug Industry, 1986.

	Pharmaceuticals	*Retail Drugs*
Return on equity	17.9%	18.2%
Return on net assets	14.5%	10.6%
Debt/equity	.23	.72
Margin	10.9%	1.9%
Turnover	1.3	5.1

Figure 4–6. Industry Performance Map.

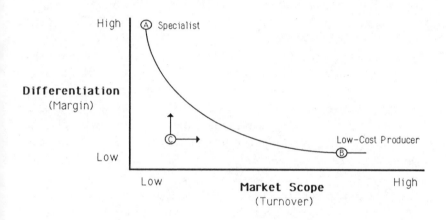

of the market, and they realize high margins as a result. Drugstores
cannot, in general, employ such a strategy. Their services are hard to
differentiate, for they merchandise the same products as other retail
druggists. As a result, profitability depends on efficient asset management (high turnover), rather than high prices.

The empirical data on industry profitability thus confirm the basic
axioms of business strategy formulation. Managers must seek to either
1) find a market segment in which their product or service is highly
differentiated (allowing higher price or affording lower cost) or, 2) maximize asset turnover by marketing their product to as large a market
as possible.

By plotting the variables of the Du Pont relationship, we can generate
the strategic relationships shown in Figure 4–6, an industry performance

map. A business can achieve high RONA by differentiating itself from the competitors (point A), which usually entails serving a narrow market segment with a unique product. But equivalent performance can be achieved by the firm at point B who successfully serves a broad segment of the market with an undifferentiated product. The winners in commodity industries fall at the lower right, the specialists win by positioning themselves at the top left. Businesses in the middle region are uncommon, since they have succeeded in spite of their position as neither the specialist nor the volume supplier.

Either strategy enhances performance. Thus, the business at point C can strive to differentiate by adding perceived value so that its products and services can be sold at higher price (a marketing-oriented approach) or it can differentiate by reducing total unit costs (an operations or manufacturing-oriented approach). Alternatively, it can increase revenue (better marketing) or reduce asset intensity.

Sometimes industry or competitive constraints prevent this freedom of choice. Looking at an industry performance map will suggest the realistic options. In the pharmaceutical industry, for example, we find substantial variation in margins because some competitors are more successful than others in introducing innovative products. The high performers in drug retailing, on the other hand, excel by better asset management. Industry performance maps thus delineate the historic perimeters of possible performance.

Every seasoned venture capital investor and most division and corporate officers can relate stories of people who have come to them with ideas for products or services that are of higher quality, more efficient, or in other ways superior to anything on the market. Naturally, the budding entrepreneur also plans to offer this fantastic new item at a lower price than anyone else. Obviously, if a strategy could be employed to increase both product differentiation (unique features, for example) and process differentiation (lower cost), business performance would be outstanding. But the unique product that everyone wants is hard to find.

Realistically, product differentiation typically increases both unit cost and fixed cost. Becoming the low-cost producer is often a long-term strategy that requires infusions of large amounts of up-front capital, and reduced short-term profit. The Japanese, for example, are reputed to have lost money on motorcycles in Europe for five years after entering the motorcycle market, but ultimately they recouped their investment and came to dominate the market. Thus, firms must decide which is a more realistic choice for them, given their situation, and follow one path or the other.

DESIGNING ELEGANT STRATEGIES

How can we recognize a good strategy? I submit that the best strategies have a subtle but crucial quality that resists quantification and rigorous definition. This inscrutable quality is *elegance.*

In mathematics and physics, elegance has long been an accepted criterion for judging a hypothesis. An elegant strategy is easy to spot. It is simple but powerful and innovative. Managers invariably get a charge out of swapping stories about original strategies that hit the jackpot. We can all think of examples from the past: In 1903 King Gillette came up with a unique strategy when he institutionalized the safety razor designed to accept only Gillette disposable razor blades. He sold the razor at cost and made money on the blades. Similarly, Xerox developed a market for its technology by renting machines to users at minimum cost and charging users 5¢ a copy.

A more recent example is the Japanese success in consumer electronics, based first on shifting the basis of competition from service to reliability, and now shifting it again to ultrashort product life cycles (as note the annual deluge of new, higher technology products). Then there's Hanes' creation of an innovative distribution system for L'Eggs pantyhose. They pioneered the sale of their product in supermarkets (implying that stockings, like eggs, are items for frequent consumption unlike other clothing, which lasts a long time), dramatically increasing brand exposure and customer convenience while bypassing direct competition from other brands stocked in traditional department stores. And Nucor's downsizing of steel mills in order to use flexibility and lower costs as a competitive edge against industry giants. And the revolutionary breaching of classic banking industry boundaries by American Express and Merrill Lynch.

We all have a longer list of crude, ill-advised strategies that flunk the aesthetics test. They lack finesse, insight, and creativity, and they often involve launching large numbers of dollars or people at the competition. Their net result is a bruising business loss at worst and meager gains at best. The oligopolistic competition in some segments of the petrochemical industry exemplifies lack of elegance.

Other crass examples include Miller's strategy to gain market share in the brewing industry, and the mindless price cutting seen during periods of excess capacity in such capital-intensive industries as chemicals, farm equipment, airlines, and large steam turbines. The endless soap wars to gain fractions of a point of market share fail the test of elegance, as does the recent rush to add diverse properties to corporate portfolios at inflated prices.

Most firms have found that they cannot buy an elegant strategy off the shelf from management consultants, and few companies have the knack of cultivating creative strategy specialists. So many businesses blunder on with implicit or explicit strategies worked out 10 or 20 years ago by their founders, but which are hardly sufficient in today's market.

Good strategies exhibit some other sterling qualities:

Informedness.   Good strategies spring from good information, from data that consider both the external environment and the internal climate of the firm. As noted earlier, a common pitfall is to base strategy on the historic performance of the business or the hopes of the managers. If this is how you plan, you're risking everything on a run of good luck.

Feasibility.   A good strategy is one that will work, provided adequate resources are assigned to it. But it is wise to remember that a good strategy is not one that produces hysteria among competitors and leads to massive punitive retaliation.

Robustness.   A good strategy is hardy. It works under a broad range of conditions. Some strategies are effective only when inflation is high, or low, or under certain transitory conditions. Although any strategy should be changed when the underlying assumptions are no longer valid, frequent changes disorient both the organization and the competitors. Above all, a robust strategy is resistant to competitors' response. If the future is important (if today's customers, suppliers, and competitors will still be in the game), then today's best strategy will strongly depend on how your competitors respond to your strategy.

Lucidity.   Good strategy is easily understood by the entire organization, which helps to assure that everyone is playing the same game. This information should be communicated clearly to your customers, who need to realize that you are making an all-out commitment to quality, or to service, or to low price. And your competitors need to know that you mean business too.

Endorsement.   The best strategies are developed with participation by all key managers and with total support by the CEO. In addition, each specific strategy within the total plan should have the enthusiastic backing of at least one senior manager, the strategy's champion.

SUMMARY

The practical strategist considers industry structure and trends, competitive position, competitors' strategy and commitment, resource availability, and risk tolerance. Critical issues to be resolved include selecting the right market segment.

The best business strategy exploits a market in which product or process differentiation can yield a major competitive advantage. This advantage will develop when a firm can reduce its input costs relative to competitors, increase its output prices, or improve its efficiency by greater productivity or scale economy.

Many strategies are available, but only a few work. The others are prone to fail because they require excessive resources, competitive retaliation occurs, or because the strategy ignores the key success factors for the industry and market segment. This is not to say that risky strategy should always be eschewed. But remember that, even when successful, the cost may exceed the benefit. Good judgment ultimately provides the balance between external constraints, the aspirations of the firm, and the risk tolerance of the managers.

The practical strategist expends most of the firm's resources on a limited number of new strategies. Five is about the most that any business can manage. Attempting to implement a larger number of strategies disperses limited resources (and managerial attention) so that no single strategy succeeds.

In the final analysis, the practical strategist applies common sense to the selection of a winning strategy. In the best cases this strategy will be elegant. But in all cases the strategy provides an advantage relative to competitors in the market segment to be served.

NOTES

1.   During the siege of Sevastopol in October 1854, Lord Cardigan led his British Light Brigade of cavalry directly into the face of the Russian field batteries. However admirable the élan of the charge, the brigade was decimated. The incident later became the subject of Alfred Lord Tennyson's epic poem.

2.   The head of a major U.S. corporation is fondly remembered for having distributed to all senior staff lapel pins asserting a corporate profit objective of $4 per share (profit at the time was approximately $2 per share). After three years, when profit had inched up by a mere 10 percent, the pins were retired with embarrassment.

3.   Some corporations make a tacit decision to withdraw, as exemplified by Montgomery Ward after World War II. By curtailing investment in suburban stores, its archconservative leader Sewell Avery allowed its major rival Sears to triple its relative size.

4.   Michael Porter has proposed three generic strategy choices: focus, low cost, and differentiation. The focus choice is a subset of the first strategy decision (selection of the market to be served). Low cost in my view is simply a subset of differentiation. See Michael E. Porter, *Competitive Strategy* (New York: The Free Press, 1980), p. 35.

5.   William K. Hall, "Survival Strategies in a Hostile Environment," *Harvard Business Review* (September/October 1980).

6.   Bowmar introduced its hand calculator in 1971 for $240 but was unable to survive against the low-cost/low-price strategies of Texas Instruments and the Japanese.

7.   According to *Atlantic Monthly* (October 1986, p. 64), 68 million children around the world spend 5 billion hours a year playing with Lego bricks.

8.   *The Competitive Status of the U.S. Auto Industry* (Washington, D.C.: National Academy Press, 1982).

9.   PIMS is a not-for-profit research project established in 1972 under the auspices of the Strategic Planning Institute in Cambridge, Massachusetts.

10. Don Collier, "Strategic Planning Systems Design and Operation," *Journal of Business Strategy* (Fall 1980).

11. Al Ries and Jack Trout, *Marketing Warfare* (New York: McGraw-Hill, 1986).

II CORPORATE STRATEGY

Business strategy considers the question of how a business should compete in the marketplace. Once a set of strategies has been proposed by the managers of the corporation's businesses, the challenge will be to articulate a strategy for the organization as a whole.

Corporate strategy addresses the issue of what industries to compete in and how to allocate resources among businesses. The central aim of this strategy will be to ensure the economic and managerial renewal of the firm. Although I know few firms have cogently and comprehensively articulated such a strategy, the task need not be approached with foreboding. As in the case of business strategy, common sense and imagination are the two prerequisites.

Why do most corporations lack a coherent corporate strategy? I attribute this deficiency to three critical factors:

1. Preoccupation with short-term financial performance
2. Not understanding what constitutes corporate strategy
3. Lack of familiarity with tools that facilitate the development of corporate strategy

We can do no more than deplore the short horizons of many corporate managers. But we address the second and third factors in Part II of this book.

The process of developing corporate strategy entails the same straightforward logic that we invoked for the formulation of business strategy; Figure II-1 presents the necessary elements of the process. The first step will be an analysis of the external and internal situation of the

Figure II-1. The Corporate Strategy Process.

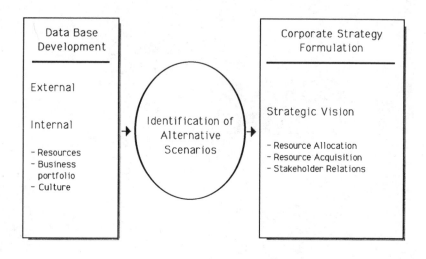

corporation, culminating in the establishment of a corporate data base. This will allow us to create a number of interesting alternative future scenarios for the corporation. Management can next identify an explicit corporate strategy that focuses attention on the attainment of one of the alternative futures.

The specific strategy decisions corporate managers must make include

- Strategic vision or dominant theme. (What will drive corporate development and renewal?)
- Resource allocation. (How will we allocate resources among existing businesses and programs, and what new investments should be made to assure the future of the corporation?)
- Resource acquisition. (How will we meet our resource requirements?)
- Stakeholder relations. (How can we best satisfy the expectations of various stakeholders?)

Part II of the *Practical Strategist* closes the gap between business strategy and corporate strategy, documenting the actions necessary to selecting practical strategy for the organization as a whole. In addition, since many corporations face the challenge of increasing industry and market globalization, developing global strategy is given special attention in Chapter 6.

5 FORMULATING CORPORATE STRATEGY

THE LOGIC OF CORPORATE STRATEGY FORMULATION

Corporate strategy is not a set of strategies describing how to compete in the marketplace. That is the domain of business strategy. Nor is corporate strategy an arbitrary statement of goals that sound challenging or the CEO's personal articulation of pious virtues or utopian future worlds. Corporate strategy in its simplest form is a description of the decisions and actions necessary to realize a particular future state for the enterprise, recognizing that a number of possible alternatives or scenarios exist.

Once a particular future has been articulated for the enterprise as a whole, a model for corporate strategy requires decisions on *resource allocation*. How corporate resources are allocated determines whether the strategic vision of the corporation can be realized. Management must also put in place a strategy for *resource acquisition* that considers how the various activities of the corporation are to be funded, how the necessary human resources are to be applied, and which other resources such as technology or manufacturing capability are needed. Finally, the corporation must establish an appropriate set of programs to assure that the needs of all the important corporate *stakeholders* have been met. The first step in formulating an overall corporate strategy, however, is to establish a good corporate data base.

THE CORPORATE DATA BASE

The corporate data base is created by assessing the pertinent external and internal conditions that exist for the corporation today and by developing an appropriate set of assumptions about expected future conditions (including the anticipated economic, social, political, and technological trends). This differs from the situation analysis performed by the individual business units, which will concentrate on assessing the market and the competition.

External Analysis

The external analysis considers all the exogenous variables and trends likely to affect the future performance of the corporation. These variables usually fall into several categories:

- *Economic.* Overall economic conditions, cost of capital, taxation policy, availability of the various factors of production, including labor and raw materials.
- *Social.* Trends in demographics, changes in cultural mores, other emerging social conditions.
- *Political.* Potential changes in the regulatory or legislative environment; local, national, or global political trends.
- *Technological.* Emerging or declining technologies, product or service innovations or alternatives.

This list is only a sample of the general factors a corporation must consider. Each organization must assess those externalities that are strategically relevant to its own future.

Trends in regulation or deregulation are often important, although government regulation is not new. The first environmental ordinance, for example, was passed in 1388 by Richard II to prohibit the fouling of waters in or near towns. The emphasis on regulation has been followed in recent years by a movement toward deregulation, part of a shift toward a more decentralized society that has profoundly affected the corporation in certain industries. Curiously, at the same time that federal regulation of most industries appears to be easing,[1] state governments anxious to protect their own revenue base and industries have taken up the slack. Recent state-sponsored bills to regulate corporate takeovers illustrate this trend.

Deregulation tends to produce a set of economic and organizational transformations that include competitive pricing, rationalization, unbundling of products and services, product proliferation, cost cutting, and earnings variability. Often these are augmented by changes in technology, increased networking, mergers and acquisitions, and organizational changes.

A loophole in the Bank Holding Company Act of 1956, for example, has allowed the formation of nonbank banks—limited service or consumer banks that either offer checking accounts or make commercial loans, but not both. The first such nonbank was created by Gulf + Western in 1980. Since then over 160 such nonbanks have been spawned by firms such as American Express, Merrill Lynch, Dreyfus, Sears, and others. These corporations have in effect entered the banking business without formally establishing banks, and the future of the 15,000 banks in the industry seems certain to be altered by this new form of competition.

While the 1970s generally represented a period of declining merger and acquisition activity, the 1980s have seen an escalation in corporate consolidation. Merger and acquisition announcements in 1986 surged to over 3,000, an 11 percent increase over 1985 and a 13-year record. The previous assumptions of low interest rates, few scale economies, and fragmented industry structure were replaced by a new set of assumptions: low inflation (verging on disinflation), high real interest rates, increased global competition, and rapid technological advances. Corporate managers responded to economic pressures by cutting costs, divesting unprofitable or unrelated operations, and strengthening core businesses. The renewed emphasis on performance and shareholders' value led to corporate restructuring, leveraged buyouts and recapitalizations, and the creation of new financing vehicles such as zero coupon and junk bonds.

A summary of major threats and opportunities facing the corporation is the natural result of the analysis of externalities. In the 1970s, for example, the heavy dependence on energy was cited by many firms as a major problem or threat to a number of their businesses, in light of the 1973 OPEC oil embargo. (Few, with the possible exception of Royal Dutch Shell, had identified energy availability or cost as a major consideration before the embargo.) In the 1980s it is not uncommon to find foreign competition appearing on many corporate lists of future threats. Opportunities often arise from the potential to apply a core corporate technology to new markets. Corning's glass technology, for example, provided easy entry to fiber optics. Entry to a new industry can also be facilitated by deregulation, as shown by the American Express expansion into financial services.

Internal Analysis

The corporation's internal analysis can usefully be divided into an assessment of its resources, including its strengths and weaknesses, and an appraisal of its values and aspirations (the corporate culture).

Resources.   What are the potential financial resources of the organization, expressed in terms of capital structure and debt capacity, market value, and cash flow (and in particular free cash)? What are the human and managerial resources? What productive physical assets are available? Does the firm have any distinctive skills or other assets such as proprietary technology? The answers to these questions will form an important part of the corporate data base.

The businesses of the firm and their strategies in themselves represent an important resource; their ability to add future economic value to the corporation must be critically evaluated. A first step, therefore, will be to examine the individual business unit plans to validate their strategies (do the proposed strategies make sense?) and the congruence of expected financial performance with strategy. Corporations often display the aggregation of corporate businesses in a format exemplified by the hypothetical seven-business portfolio of Figure 5–1 (circle size represents relative revenue). Alternative formats (for example the 3×3 industry attractiveness/business strength display) may be equally revealing.

The overall *strategic* condition of the corporate portfolio will suggest the need for corporate actions that typically include one or more of the following:

- Increase growth.
- Change economic balance (for example, cyclicity).
- Improve competitive strength.
- Redeploy assets to more attractive industries.
- Maintain the current configuration.

Appraising the feasibility of portfolio change represents one of the principal challenges in the corporate strategy process, since assets cannot easily be moved around the corporate game board. For example,

Figure 5–1. A Typical Corporate Portfolio of Businesses.

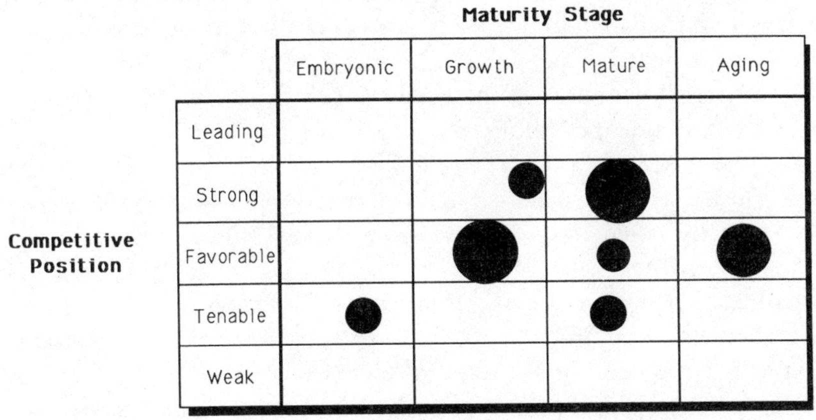

		Maturity Stage			
		Embryonic	Growth	Mature	Aging
	Leading				
	Strong		●	●	
Competitive Position	Favorable		●	●	●
	Tenable	●		●	
	Weak				

Allied Chemical's corporate portfolio in 1981 showed a preponderance of mature businesses and a corresponding paucity of businesses in the early growth stage. This imbalance encouraged Hennessy, Allied's new CEO, to commit significant resources to high technology (a strategy intended to yield slow improvements in the portfolio) and to growth by acquisition (a rapid change strategy). Between 1981 and 1985, the Allied tripled its corporate R&D budget and launched a major acquisition thrust that culminated in the purchase of Eltra, Fisher Scientific, Instrumentation Laboratories, Bendix, and Signal.

The *financial* condition of a corporate portfolio will highlight particular problems in sales, profits, or asset distribution. Essential information is the overall flow of cash within the corporation, a display of source and use of funds disaggregated to the business unit level. Typical corporate objectives that derive from these analyses include:

• Improve profitability.
• Adjust internal cash flow.
• Reduce risk.

Corporate Culture.   After resources have been assessed, it is time to evaluate the organization's values and aspirations. Interest in corporate culture is relatively new, although the McKinsey 7-S model presaged current interest in a systemic approach to management (the seven elements are structure, systems, style, staff, skills, strategy, and shared values). Despite the recent publicity given to corporate culture, it remains an elusive and uncomfortable concept for most corporate executives. Yet the values and norms of the organization dominate its decisions not only on what strategy makes sense but also how to implement it. Consensus needs to be reached on the current culture and whether it constrains or energizes the organization in its evolution.

We may define the culture of an organization as a *set of shared beliefs and values* or alternatively as *a pattern of learned behavior.* The value set will include attitudes toward risk and time, toward stakeholders (the priority assigned to satisfying shareholders, customers, employees), and performance priorities (for example, revenue growth versus profit, financial performance versus nonfinancial performance). As in any social system, a number of conflicts usually appear as managers attempt to manage the trade-offs between growth and stability and balance the needs of the organization versus the needs of its members.

Different industries are usually characterized by different sets of values. A small new venture in computer software, for example, has a short time horizon, high tolerance for risk, and primary emphasis on the interest of the owner-managers; growth and market share are important measures of its performance. A bank, on the other hand, has a long time horizon, lower tolerance for risk, and an emphasis on customers' welfare. Continuity and growth of dividends are key performance measures for banks.

Different cultures are also found within a particular industry. The contrasts between IBM (disciplined, centralized) and Apple (entrepreneurial, decentralized), Texas Instruments (market share is a virtue, so drive down the cost) and Hewlett-Packard (product quality is a virtue, so market a highly engineered product at premium price) illustrate this diversity and explain the different strategies adopted by the firms. But it is not unusual to find dramatically different cultures (subcultures) within the same organization; witness, for example, the classic polarization between marketing and production.

Strategy is often congruent with culture. Unfortunately, however, firms sometimes select strategies that are not. Strategies that violate organizational norms fail to muster organizational commitment and are extremely difficult to implement. In other words, they are risky. Thus, as illustrated by Figure 5–2, risk is minimized if a strategy is not only competitively sound but also compatible with the cultural norms of the organization.

For example, a firm competing in a growth industry may wish to expand its market share. Achieving this objective by acquisition may

Figure 5-2.   Strategic and Cultural Congruence.

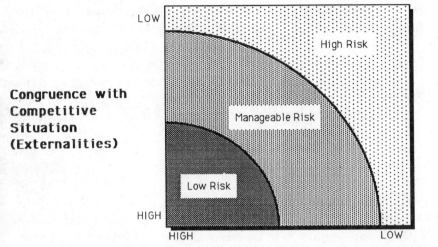

**Congruence with
Competitive
Situation
(Externalities)**

**Congruence with Organizational Norms
(Internalities)**

not be viable if the firm has no history of successfully seeking and consummating acquisitions, especially if the corporation has difficulty integrating outsiders. Firms in regulated industries such as telephone and banking continue to experience great difficulty in adopting strategies in which marketing and competition are the norm.

Many examples of mismatch between strategy and culture can be found in the electric utility industry. Until the early 1970s the industry enjoyed steady growth in demand (doubling every 10 years). Customers were placid. Shareholders looked forward with confidence to consistent dividends. Regulatory proceedings were mere formalities. Resource availability was not an issue, and the fossil fuel technology looked viable for many years. Suddenly, after the 1973 oil embargo, demand for power in most sections of the country fell to less than 2 percent per year. Fossil technology was abandoned by many firms as they rushed to place orders for nuclear systems that promised lower fuel costs. Once-passive stakeholders began to assert themselves on issues of acid rain, plant siting, nuclear risk, rate increases, and poor service. The tranquil regulatory process and speedy approval of licenses or rate changes became contentious adversary proceedings.

The environment had changed and the strategies selected earlier were no longer appropriate. But the culture built up in many utilities over 50 years of stability had immobilized them. The cautious, conservative management style that so comfortably enabled them to earn high returns was no longer appropriate and dramatically delayed their response to crisis. The result was a period of tribulation that persists even today. The consequences have included bond default (Washington Public Power Supply), plant abandonment (Indiana), bankruptcy (Public Service of New Hampshire), and fraud litigation (Long Island Lighting).

Practical strategists need to understand how the fabric of the organization affects its ability to respond to change and to implement new strategy. They must also consider a corporation's ability even to identify strategic options.[2] The first task then is diagnostic: What is the culture? Regrettably, the values of an organization are often difficult to identify, since they cannot be observed directly. Following the methods of classical anthropology, however, we can characterize a corporation's culture by studying the behavior of managers and other employees. Many dimensions of culture can be derived from an audit of the firm's goals (profit or growth?), time horizons (long or short?), heroes or heroines, ceremonies or rituals, rewards (monetary or psychic?), communications (informal or formal?) and so forth.

If the organization's strategy and culture are mutually supportive, implementation can move forward. If strategy and culture are incompatible, managers must either change the strategy or change the culture. Unfortunately, many managers resist evolution, and change in culture almost always occurs slowly, over a period of many years. The dynamics of the process are described clearly in one model propounded by social psychologist Kurt Lewin. He describes the organization as fixed (frozen) in place by a set of external and internal forces. To move to a new position (to change the culture), we must unfreeze the organization by removing these constraining forces. The organization can then be repositioned, where appropriate constraints are again applied to maintain stability.

Most organizations in crisis will adapt to new conditions by modifying their behavior only after they have identified a new dominant theme or vision (Figure 5–3). Corporations that maintain high performance over a sustained period of time are able to sense the need for new leadership and new visions. After the new vision has been enunciated and institutionalized, implementation of more suitable strategies can begin, and performance will improve. This process of adaptation can be observed at 3M (Lehr succeeded by Jacobson), Allied (Connors succeeded by Hennessy), GE (Jones succeeded by Welch), and Chrysler (Iacocca). The managerial evolution in Xerox from Wilson (the entrepreneur) to McColough (the bureaucrat) to Kearns (the rejuvenator) offers another useful case history.[3]

Cultural change requires an openness to new ways of perceiving the world and responding to it.[4] But managers frequently deny reality both before and during a crisis. In some situations therefore, a commissar may be a more appropriate change agent than a yogi, to invoke Arthur Koestler's metaphor.[5] In other words, rapid (sometimes traumatic) change, including significant changes in personnel, may be the best prescription for metanoia, or transformation. Evolutionary change may not be fast enough to ensure the survival of the firm.

IDENTIFYING ALTERNATIVE SCENARIOS

The corporate data bank will contribute an assessment of the organization's external and internal environments and its strengths, opportunities, weaknesses, and threats. Management can next begin to construct several alternative scenarios. These scenarios will depict the desirable position and configuration of the organization at the end of a certain time horizon, perhaps 5–10 years (although a longer time horizon may

Figure 5–3. Cultural Transformation and Performance.

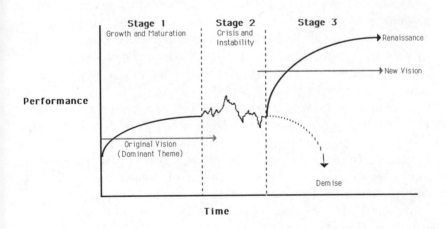

be appropriate for industries like forest products or electric power generation). Parameters that are usually specified in such a scenario include size, profitability, served markets or industries, and portfolio composition. The resources required to realize different scenarios need not be addressed at this stage of the process.

The concept of scenarios to develop surprise-free alternative futures was popularized by Kahn and Wiener.[6] They define a scenario as a hypothetical sequence of events constructed for the purpose of focusing attention on causal processes and decision points. Thus, scenarios are not forecasts, but rather a means of improving our understanding of the possible long-term consequences of trends, policies, and their interaction.

The scenario process has profound historical legitimacy, dating back to the Chinese I Ching, the oracles of Greece (the most famous of which was perhaps the oracle of Apollo at Delphi), and the Tarot. More contemporary technology for constructing scenarios includes expert opinion, cross-impact analysis, and computer modeling. Both important world models[7] produced during the 1970s under the sponsorship of the Club of Rome were the result of a computer-based approach to scenarios based on the Systems Dynamics work carried out by Jay Forrester and his associates at MIT. The best recent examples of the application of scenarios can probably be found at Royal Dutch Shell.[8]

Formulating scenarios for corporate strategy is an opportunity for managers to be creative. Although a corporation's history imposes strong (and sometimes ineffable) constraints[9] on its ability or willingness to change course, nevertheless, the future of an organization does not need to be like its past, which is why we encourage managers to examine a full range of options before selecting one. Managers need to take advantage of the opportunity to design their own futures and to tell interesting stories about how their corporations might evolve.[10] An organization might choose growth, diversification, or the maintenance of its present condition as its goal.

There may be no single ideal future, for managers will make subjective judgments about how to satisfy the needs of the various constituencies they represent. Moreover, one manager will perceive the world differently from another (have a separate reality or *Weltanschauung*) and place different values on particular outcomes (have a different utility function). Even if we agree that the long-range objective is to maximize the shareholder's value, the strategy options may require trade-offs. Thus, continued growth may entail diversification with high risk and loss of corporate identity. But failure to grow may result in lower market value, vulnerability to takeover, and managerial atrophy or ennui.

Furthermore, what is beneficial for one corporation may be disastrous for another, and each organization must seek its own Camelot or Ultima Thule. American Can (now Primerica), for example, has abandoned the packaging industry, but firms like Weyerhaeuser and Triangle continue to invest enthusiastically in this same industry.

In many instances, an organization can undergo a metastasis—a significant change in position, shape, or form without changing its core business; IBM is perhaps the best example. Occasionally, as we have often seen in recent times, a corporation asserts that diversity is an important aspect of its future scenario, particularly if most of its assets have been dedicated to a single volatile or cyclical industry, or if, like the conglomerates, financial balance is an overarching theme for the firm.

The development of a corporate data base and the articulation of alternative future scenarios for the corporation represent the prelude to selection of specific corporate strategies.

SELECTING CORPORATE STRATEGY

Vision and Dominant Theme

Corporate strategy is the expression of the future state toward which the organization strives, a statement of what the firm wants to do and what the firm wants to become—the corporation's *vision*. The vision, in other words, represents a single scenario selected from among the several that may have been identified. Corporate strategy describes how the corporation will realize the future scenario or strategic vision it has chosen.

Corporations having clear strategic visions usually have identified a *dominant theme*—a leitmotif, or a singular orientation toward an industry, technology, or set of managerial skills.[11] Where do strategic visions and dominant themes come from? They often emerge, rather than springing forth out of the void. The classic model for the creative process applies. A sustained stage of data gathering and analysis precedes a stage of incubation, which ultimately leads to illumination, the stage of insight and awareness of the solution.

A strong dominant theme (be it implicit or explicit) provides focus and serves as a plumbline for managerial behavior. Historic exemplars of dominant themes, now abandoned, include Du Pont ("Better things for better living through chemistry") and AT&T ("Universal service"). Noncorporate exemplars have included the Catholic Church, the Green Bay Packers, and the Boston Celtics. As specific recent expressions of dominant themes we might cite the following:

> A renewed commitment to our simply stated goal of making the fastest, most powerful computers there are—period. [Cray Research]

> Over the next five years, Beatrice will emerge as the world's premier marketer of food and consumer products . . . the power in the consumer marketplace, wherever we choose to compete . . . Our first priority will be total dedication to anticipating and satisfying consumer needs.

> The personal computer is the heart of Apple. . . We have just one goal: to lead the industry in innovation. For those who use personal computers daily—and especially for the millions who have never used a personal computer—we want to provide the most flexible and technologically advanced computer solutions available.

> C&C, the integration of computers and communications to meet diversified needs in worldwide markets. [NEC Corporation]

A dominant theme or corporate purpose often changes as the firm's self-image evolves. Thus Bic moved from a ballpoint pen manufacturer to purveyor of writing instruments and ultimately to consumer goods company. Diversity in itself tends to blur the dominant theme, although even extreme diversity can be defined and justified in particular ways, as witness GE's latest three-circle expression of the unity of the corporation's endeavors (Figure 5–4). Using this model, GE's 14 key businesses are grouped into a set of technology businesses, service businesses, and core manufacturing businesses, all supported by five support operations. The overlap of the three major circles implies (or perhaps suggests the desire for) synergy among the business groups.

In 1985 Allied attempted to impose a similar logic on its diversity, to position itself for the next era in its evolution. By acquiring the Signal Corporation, it completed the strategy begun in the Hennessy era of focusing on three core high-technology businesses: aerospace/electronics, automotive, and engineered materials. The corporation's 35 "nonstrategic" businesses were then spun off into a new public company (the Henley Group), whose shares were distributed to existing shareholders as a dividend, Allied retaining 30 percent of the equity.

Unfortunately, a powerful dominant theme is a necessary but not a sufficient precursor to corporate success. For example, the recent commitment by the Allegis companies (United Airlines, Hertz rental

Figure 5–4.   General Electric's 1986 Portfolio.

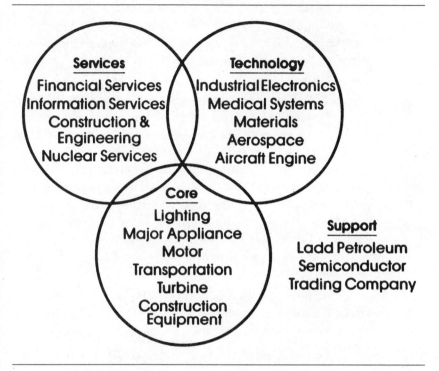

cars, and Westin Hotels) to ''Caring for travellers worldwide'' did not enthuse the various stockholders, who forced a restructuring.

The vision and dominant theme are often expressed in the form of an explicit *mission statement* for the corporation, which forms an integral part of the corporate strategy. Regrettably, most such statements are just trite rephrasings (in the corporate idiom) of the ten commandments or the Boy Scouts' oath. Strategic visions should be exciting, inspirational, and empowering. They should compel managers to change their corporation in whatever manner is required to enable the vision or future scenario to be realized.

A meaningful mission statement displays the following qualities:[12]

- Expresses the future scope of the firm's activities. The arenas or industries and markets in which the firm has chosen to participate should be clearly defined.

- Differentiates the organization from other organizations. Being profitable, producing quality products, treating employees fairly—these are the platitudes embraced by all companies. A mission statement should do more. It should speak to the specific identity of the organization, the degree to which the organization is unique.

- Articulates the relevance to all the meaningful constituencies of the firm. One stakeholder group may be assigned primacy (for example, the investors), but all must be addressed. The organization that slights another stakeholder group walks a perilous path. The indifference of electric utilities such as Long Island Lighting and Boston Edison to the communities surrounding their proposed nuclear plants, for example, created costly construction delays for management. The bland assumption by the trustees of Gallaudet University in 1988 that they could appoint a nondeaf president infuriated the students, who successfully sought her resignation.

- Reveals objectives in a way that allows the corporation to measure progress toward them. Parameters like growth, size, profitability, and diversity need to be made explicit.

The specific actions to be taken by the corporation (that is, the corporate strategy) fall into three categories: resource allocation, resource acquisition, and stakeholder relations.

Resource Allocation

The resources of the corporation must be allocated to strategies that lead in the right direction—toward attainment of the corporate vision. This requires responses to numerous difficult questions. How are resources to be allocated among the businesses of the corporation; which opportunities should be given priority? Is disposition of existing assets or acquisition of new assets desirable? Which new industries are attractive? What support will be given to the corporation's resource centers? What new corporate projects need to be funded? How will the strategies to be supported combine to create leverage?

In an enlightened organization, resources are allocated to business strategies that will add economic and strategic value to the firm. Unfortunately, the internal redistribution of resources in an organization tends to evolve slowly, despite the inevitable scarcity of resources. Thus, managers often discover that only new corporate resources are available for contention and that existing resources tend to be assigned to the same managers or strategies (even if they are cash traps), probably on grounds that the sunk investment needs to be recovered. Said in another way, even though the current allocations may be recognized as unsatisfactory, barriers may be too great to make instantaneous changes. A firm, for example, cannot instantaneously open or close a manufacturing plant, start or stop a major research program, exit or enter an industry.

Nonetheless, the proper starting point for the allocation of resources is the identification of attractive industries for corporate investment. A selected list of criteria follows, but each organization must develop its own.

Criteria for Assessing Industry Attractiveness
- Size
- Market growth
- Market diversity/customer concentration
- Financial viability of customers
- Cyclicity or seasonality
- Competitive structure
- Entry barriers
- Industry profitability
- Social values
- Environmental constraints
- Regulatory forces
- Inflation vulnerability
- Labor intensity
- Energy intensity
- Capital intensity
- Technological intensity
- Supplier power or resource availability
- Human resource needs
- Fit with distinctive competence

The ranking of criteria will always be a subjective reflection of the history of the firm. Thus, firms with primary experience in serving industrial markets tend to avoid consumer markets, and cash-poor firms shun capital-intensive industries. The firm's value system also affects the ranking. For example, in reviewing possible diversification into broadcasting, the chairman of a major telecommunications corporation observed to his staff that such a move was unthinkable. Not, to be sure, because the industry was unprofitable, but rather because "I've met those executives, and they're not like us" (and he was right).

Ultimately the corporation will be faced with two options: to redistribute resources internally or to allocate resources to new activities—that is, to diversify.

Internal Redistribution.   The simple logic of allocating resources within the corporation will suggest that resources be allocated liberally to those businesses that do have priority and withheld from those that do not. For the corporation having but a single business in an attractive industry, the resource allocation decision is straightforward. But the decision for multibusiness corporations is more of a challenge. Unfortunately, many corporations allocate resources on the basis of historic patterns, corporate politics, or a mechanical application of hurdle rates. The appropriate principle to be observed is that resources be allocated to strategies (rather than to projects or to managers).

One model to facilitate the allocation process is shown in Figure 5–5. The corporation invests aggressively to build market position in high priority, Category I businesses. Selective investment to build position or improve profitability is made in Category II and III businesses, while low-priority businesses are candidates for disinvestment. An analogous set of resource allocation guidelines is shown in Table 5–1. In any situation, however, practical strategists examine particular businesses and their individual potentials, rather than follow general guidelines by rote. Thus, a corporation may realize that it *must* establish a position in an industry in which it has no current activity.

We can test the rationality of the allocation decisions by examining how the free cash of the corporation is distributed internally. High-priority businesses will use cash, either because they are attempting to achieve rapid growth or because they wish to improve their competitive position. Low-priority businesses, on the other hand, will throw off cash, either because they are mature and do not need cash or because they have begun to harvest their position.

From an economic point of view, resources must always be allocated so that the marginal returns exceed the marginal cost of capital. To increase the shareholder's value, in fact, the return on equity (ROE) must always be greater than the cost of equity capital (k_e). This argues for setting a different hurdle rate for each business to reflect its risk. In effect, then, the corporation demands a greater return from its high-risk businesses than from its low-risk businesses.

Figure 5–5. A Model for Allocating Internal Resources.

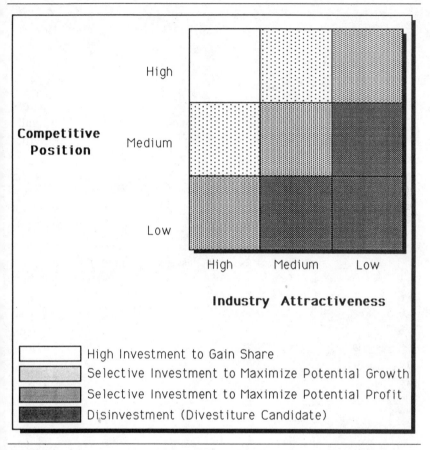

Although few corporations are so sophisticated, beta (β) and the cost of capital can be estimated for the business units within a corporation by either simulation or peer group comparisons. For an investment with no risk such as government securities, β, a standard measure of volatility or risk, is equal to zero. When the risk increases, investors seek a premium on their expected returns. The risk premium for the stockmarket as a whole ($\beta = 1$) is estimated to be approximately 6 percent.

Hergert has used peer-group analysis to estimate β and the cost of capital for a hypothetical diversified corporation comprising Hoover (home appliances), Cincinnati Milacron (machine tools), and U.S. Tobacco (tobacco).[13] As expected, both β and the cost of equity capital differ significantly from division to division. The machine tool division has

Table 5-1. Guidelines for Resource Allocation to Business Units.

	Embryonic	Growth	Early Mature	Late Mature
Leadership	*Maintain competitive position* Increase market share Invest to lead market demand Cash user; may be profitable	*Maintain competitive position* Hold market share Invest to sustain growth Cash producer; profitable	*Maintain competitive position* Grow with industry Invest as needed Cash producer; profitable	*Maintain competitive position* Reinvest as needed Cash producer; profitable
Strong	*Improve competitive position* Increase market share Invest proportional to market demand Cash user; marginal profits	*Improve competitive position* Increase market share Invest to increase growth Cash user; probably profitable	*Maintain competitive position* Grow with industry Invest as needed Cash producer; profitable	*Maintain position or harvest* Minimum investment Cash producer; profitable
Favorable	*Improve position selectively* Increase share in specific markets Invest selectively Cash user; probably unprofitable	*Improve competitive position* Increase share selectively Invest selectively Cash user; marginal profits	*Maintain competitive position* Identify and protect niche Selective investment Cash producer; modest profits	*Harvest or withdraw* Maintain or disinvest Cash balance; moderate profits
Tenable	*Improve position selectively* Increase share very selectively Invest selectively Cash user; unprofitable	*Improve competitive position* Identify and protect niche Invest selectively Cash user; unprofitable	*Maintain position or harvest* Minimum investment or disinvestment Cash balance; minimum profits	*Withdraw or abandon* Disinvest or divest Cash balance; minimum profits
Weak	*Up or out* Invest or divest Cash user; unprofitable	*Turn around or abandon* Invest or divest Cash user; unprofitable	*Turn around or withdraw* Selective investment or disinvestment Cash user; unprofitable	*Abandon* Divest Unprofitable

the highest β (1.42), reflecting its sensitivity to the economy; its cost of capital of 15.0 percent is 4.7 percent greater than the 10.3 percent cost for relatively stable tobacco business (β = 0.73).

In some situations a dramatic reallocation of funds within the corporation will be required to produce expected results that are consistent with the strategic vision of the corporation. Examples of this situation occur when the firm's existing business portfolio is too weak, too mature, too risky, or unattractive along other dimensions.

The challenge of sustaining corporate growth, for example, is dramatically shown in Table 5–2, which compares the 10 largest U.S. manufacturing firms in 1917 with the 10 leaders in 1987. (Can you identify the ten 1917 leaders before looking at the table?) Only four of the largest firms in 1917 remain on the list in 1987 (Exxon, Ford, Du Pont, and GE). Several have been acquired (Swift by Esmark, Armour by Greyhound), and three have changed name (American Sugar is now Amstar, American Smelting is now Asarco, and Standard Oil is now Exxon).

U.S. Steel was the leader in 1917 with sales of $1.285 billion (and net income of $224 million!). But it has fallen to fifteenth place with a mere $18 billion in sales (a real compound annual growth rate from 1917 to 1985 of 0.66 percent) and recently changed its name to USX to reflect its growing diversified interests in chemicals, real estate, and oil. The smallest manufacturing firm in the 1987 Fortune 500 (M.A. Hanna) sold over $400 million of product and would have qualified for the top 10 in 1917.

Table 5–2.   America's Top 10 Manufacturers, Ranked by Sales Volume, $M.

1917	Sales	1987	Sales
1. U.S. Steel[a]	$1,285	1. General Motors	$101,782
2. Swift	875	2. Exxon	76,416
3. Armour[b]	577	3. Ford Motor	71,643
4. American Smelting[c]	441	4. IBM	54,217
5. Standard Oil (New Jersey)[d]	412	5. Mobil	51,223
6. Bethlehem Steel	299	6. General Electric	39,315
7. Ford Motor	275	7. Texaco	34,372
8. DuPont	270	8. AT&T	33,598
9. American Sugar Refining[e]	200	9. DuPont	30,468
10. General Electric	197	10. Chrysler	26,257

[a]Now USX.
[b]Now part of Greyhound.
[c]Now Asarco.
[d]Now Exxon.
[e]Now Amstar.

What do these data imply for the manager? It is apparent, first of all, that economic demand changes; only automobiles and oil have remained in fashion over a 70-year time span. A corporation's managers who positioned their firms in the "wrong" industry were doomed to experience declining demand for their product. If growth is an important corporate objective, the alternative to clairvoyance would appear to be diversification, a strategy applied with some success by GE, Bic, and American Can. But diversification is a risky solution to the dilemma of low growth or a flawed portfolio.

Diversification.   The corporation faced with the prospect of declining growth turns frequently to diversification by either internal development or acquisition, depending on the history of the corporation and the personality of its leadership. Not surprisingly, a substantial body of research demonstrates that diversity among the businesses in a corporation can be a curse unless they share common resources and thereby achieve synergy or reduce corporate costs.[14] In his classic 1974 study of 246 firms, Rumelt adopted a typology that recognized four diversification modes for a corporation:[15]

Single business. More than 95 percent of corporate revenue is derived from the base business.
Dominant business. Between 70 and 95 percent of corporate revenue is from the base business.
Related businesses. Less than 70 percent revenue is from the base business, but diversification is related by market, distribution, product, or R&D.
Unrelated. More than 30 percent revenue is from unrelated business.

Rumelt found that higher returns on sales and capital are realized by firms that engage in related diversification rather than unrelated diversification.[16] He concluded, moreover, that performance differences were highly dependent on the way that the diversity was managed. Subsequent studies confirm that the choice of industry can also significantly influence profitability.[17]

Successful diversification requires first that the corporation find an attractive industry. Unfortunately, entry into an attractive industry requires a premium, for entry barriers are usually high. Acquisition of an attractive company within that industry demands still an additional premium. Successful entry by internal development, by contrast, requires patient capital, good timing, persistence, and high tolerance on the part of management for the quirks of entrepreneurs.

Firms like 3M prefer to rely on the creativity of R&D staff to generate new business opportunities from within, a strategy that is reinforced by the introversion of the corporation and its suspicion of outsiders—its difficulty in communicating with managers who do not share the 3M view of the world. Allied-Signal in recent years has relied heavily on acquisition, a legacy of Hennessy's formative years under Geneen at ITT and Gray at United Technologies. General Electric has turned from internal development to acquisition in response to Welch's recent appetite for rapid growth. But both internal development and acquisition present major pitfalls.

Internal Development.   If the corporation has a reservoir of technology or competence in a particular functional area, internal development is a logical choice for achieving diversity. But success may come slowly and infrequently. Although overall sensitivity to market needs has improved the success rate in recent years, the performance statistics are still sobering. Only one of every 7 new product ideas becomes a commercial success (Figure 5–6). Many projects fail in the laboratory. But a larger number fail because a market is not effectively developed, however wondrous the technical achievement.

Biggadike's data show that new ventures on average do not become profitable until after the eighth year of their existence.[18] And some never make it, as witness Singer's 10-year (1965–1975) attempt to establish a new venture in business machines and GE's abortive 13-year effort (1957–1970) to enter the computer industry. The Miller case (described in the Appendix A to this chapter) serves as a classic example of how even a strategically successful diversification can be an economic disaster.

RCA also strove for many years to establish itself in the general purpose computer business. Laboring under the delusion that technology and cash were the name of the game, they aimed at the number 2 position in the industry and a 10 percent market share. But in September 1971 they conceded failure and sold their customer base to Univac. Nearly 8,000 people lost their jobs, and RCA took a $490 million write-off, the largest since Ford's $250 million write-off for the Edsel.

Babcock and Wilcox's (B&W) experiment in diversification outside of boilermaking is equally egregious. Faced with a five-year history of flat sales in his core business, B&W's chairman Morris Nielsen decided that a shift into the manufacture of nuclear pressure vessels would

Figure 5–6. Mortality of New Product Ideas.

THE NUMBER OF NEW PRODUCT IDEAS CONSIDERED TO DEVELOP ONE SUCCESSFUL NEW PRODUCT HAS BEEN REDUCED FROM 58 TO 7 – REFLECTING INCREASED PRESCREENING AND PLANNING

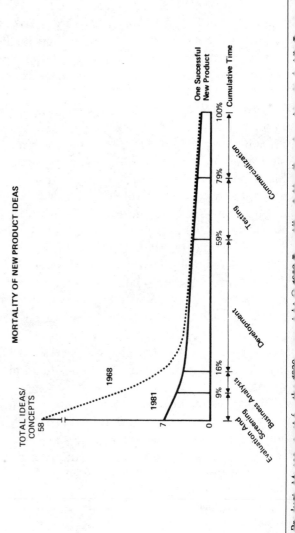

MORTALITY OF NEW PRODUCT IDEAS

offer a logical cure. In 1965 he opened a new plant in Mount Vernon, Indiana, a farm town on the Ohio River selected because of its "unspoiled labor market." The 70-foot pressure vessels with their 18-inch wall thicknesses bore little resemblance to conventional boiler pressure vessels, and the customers' quality requirements were far more rigorous. B&W expected an easy transfer of technology, however, and introduced automated manufacturing lines and new quality control equipment, including linear accelerators.

But the workers proved intransigent and "untrainable" despite a massive educational program. Labor disputes escalated. The new equipment did not work, and the rejection rate on welds soared to 70 percent. By 1968 all 28 vessels in the plant were behind schedule, some by as much as 17 months. Paul Craven, division vice president, watched helplessly as decisions continued to be made for him by B&W's corporate offices, and the situation deteriorated. In October 1968 Craven committed suicide. Customers began litigation, and costs mounted. B&W's earnings in 1969 ultimately fell from $2.00 to $0.30 per share, the stock plummeted from $40 to $20 per share, and the subsequent recovery took five years.

Acquisition.   The recent acquisition experience of U.S. firms has been a disappointment to many corporate architects of this strategy, not to mention the corporate shareholders. Combustion Engineering invested $545 million in a series of high-technology acquisitions that collectively returned only $20 million in 1968 in pretax earnings. Armco, Gould, McDonnell Douglas, Exxon, and others have similarly suffered the consequences of unsuccessful acquisition. Other major acquisition catastrophes of the past 10 years include Mobil's takeover of Marcor, GE's acquisition of Utah International, and Philip Morris's purchase of 7-Up.[19] Scherer concludes from a study of 6,000 acquisitions between 1950 and 1976 that no significant improvement in performance takes place after an acquisition; on average, the businesses continued to underperform their competitors.[20]

Nonetheless, according to a recent study the value of mergers and acquisitions in 1986 amounted to a record $190 billion.[21] To put this sum in perspective, the monies spent in acquiring over 2,500 new businesses substantially exceeded the combined expenditures in 1986 for R&D and nonresidential investment.

Although acquisition fever still rages, fewer good candidates are available, except in industries such as banking and telecommunications, where deregulation has created new opportunities. To avoid the possibility of takeover, many medium-sized firms have gone private. At the same time the strong market has raised the price of many acquisitions to the point beyond which they make good business sense; premiums averaging 50 percent over market value were paid in 1979. Average premiums had declined to 38 percent over market value by 1986, but the average price/earnings multiple paid increased from 14.3 in 1979 to 22.2 in 1986.[22] And premiums were higher in growth or glamor industries. Transaction costs also escalated, although this has reduced the incidence of hostile takeovers.

Some acquisition programs do work. All of McGraw-Hill's businesses over a 100-year period were acquired. GE has fueled much of its growth through acquisition, although its acquisition activity was balanced by an even more aggressive divestiture program. And Dun and Bradstreet generated over 80 percent of its 1986 revenue from acquisitions made over a 25-year period. American Can's redeployment of assets from packaging to financial services has apparently been successful as well, although it is too early to make final judgment.

White Consolidated made seven successful acquisitions in the 1970s, including the appliance assets of Gibson, Kelvinator, Bendix, Athens, Westinghouse, Ford, and Frigidaire. In many cases a losing property was purchased at below book value (for example, the Westinghouse business was purchased at a 42 percent discount from book value) and made profitable within a year or two. But few corporations are equipped to successfully carry out an acquisition program so clearly defined and singleminded. For that matter few such opportunities exist, particularly in the mid-1980s when valuations are so high.

Many apparent acquisition-divestiture anomalies (why does one corporation buy what another corporation is selling?) can be explained if we recognize that a certain business may have more value to one corporation than to another. Thus GE disposed of its small appliance operations because it believed that a leadership position in this industry had little value—resources would be better deployed in support of businesses in other industries. Black & Decker was a willing acquirer because it saw a fit between small appliances and its power tool activities and an opportunity to develop synergy. Gillette sold its Cricket lighter business because it saw little opportunity for future profitability. But to a Swedish Match, the acquiring corporation, the Cricket product offered an entry to the U.S. market and the chance to strengthen its position worldwide. Thomson bartered its medical imaging business to GE in exchange for GE's consumer electronic business; Thomson strives for size and reduced dependence on a small number of markets, while GE triples market share in Europe and gains access to new technologies.

Keys to Successful Diversification.   How can firms diversify with greater assurance of success? Observing these three principles can help increase the odds of success:

1.   Select an attractive industry.
2.   Pay fair value.
3.   Integrate carefully.

Most diversifications disappoint their sponsors because one or more of these caveats are ignored. Although acquisition failures get more publicity, internal development failures are equally numerous. They are just easier to sweep under the corporate rug.

1. Attractive industry.   An attractive industry almost invariably offers an opportunity to apply the firm's distinctive competence. But a superficial conclusion that distinctive competence can be extended into a new industry may be risky. Philip Morris failed in its attempt to apply consumer marketing skills to the management of 7-Up. And both Polaroid and 3M stumbled when they attempted to diversify from their specialty-product, high-margin arenas into the cut throat commodity business of audio/video tape.

Heublein made an abortive attempt to apply skills developed in its successful vodka business to the marketing of Hamm's beer. But regional marketing and distributing of downscale beer is not the same as marketing and distributing a premium distilled spirit on a national basis. Furthermore, Heublein lacked or overlooked the importance of manufacturing skills in the brewing industry. Heublein finally took a $20 million capital loss when it sold Hamm's to a group of local distributors after 10 years of unprofitable operation. (The new management has since prospered by refocusing marketing efforts on local customers.)

If diversification by acquisition is the chosen strategy, a set of formal guidelines is indispensable. Otherwise, corporate management will be harassed mercilessly by investment bankers and other merchants who offer a variety of deals, few of which may satisfy the strategic needs of the corporation. Formal criteria make possible a quick screening of apparent opportunities, permitting management to concentrate on the true opportunities. A good practical set of guidelines has been developed by Westinghouse:[23]

- Must guidelines
  Create value.
  Be manageable by Westinghouse.
  Be compatible with Westinghouse's quality standards.
  Do not expose the corporation to open-ended liabilities.
- Want guidelines
  Served market growing faster than gross national product.
  Be (or have the potential to become) a major player.
  Relate to an existing business.
  Keep total cost as low as principal competitors' cost.
  Return on equity able to approach 18–21 percent corporate target.

2. Fair value.   Many industries are attractive because high barriers deter entry of new competitors. Entry by internal development may take a long time and be costly as well as risky. Buying the leader in an attractive industry, on the other hand, may necessitate payment of an exorbitant premium. If the price is too high, the firm will never realize a satisfactory return on its investment.

An acquisition map (Figure 5–7) can be a helpful guide to valuation.[24] In general, strong firms that are profitable [D] are too expensive. Profitable firms that are strategically weak [A] are soufflés—their value may collapse. Firms that have neither strategic nor operational virtues [B] are losers—to be avoided at any price. The best deal will be a strategically positioned firm [C] that needs operational control to improve performance, although the pitfalls of turnarounds are well known.

3. Integration.   This principle invokes all the historic admonitions about the importance of synergy or field strength. An acquiring company must be prepared to contribute to the company being sought, as opposed to expecting the acquired firm to contribute all the value.

Thus, a long-range plan for integration of acquisitions is essential. Assuming that the two firms have a cultural or temperamental fit may be risky. Lack of fit for many diversifications may lead to irremediable clashes of culture, as precipitated Roger Smith's difficulty in coping at General Motors with the intransigence of an entrepreneurial Ross Perot. Only 18 months after the acquisition of his EDS computer firm for $2.5 billion, Perot was personally bought out of his GM holdings for the princely sum of $701 million.

Figure 5–7. Acquisition Audit Map.

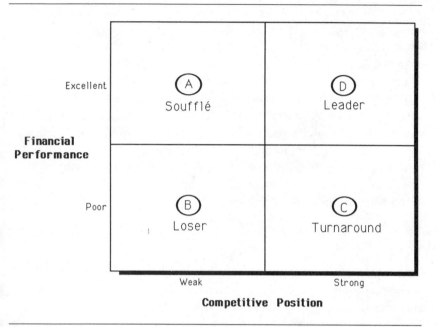

Integration can be expedited by a careful program of mutual education and cross transfer (preferably promotions) across company boundaries. Regardless of the benevolence of the new environment, some top managers will leave (not relishing the prospect of demotion to run divisions or departments). Therefore, a contingency plan to deal with their departure is important.

For some firms, diversification makes no sense. The regional Bell operating companies (RBOCs) are enjoined by law from generating more than 10 percent of their revenues from unrelated businesses (that is, they cannot cross–subsidize). And the 1982 AT&T settlement also specifically prohibited significant participation in long-distance service, manufacturing, or information services industries. This regulation probably spares the shareholders some of the pain experienced as corporations try to learn about a new industry, but it opens the market to opportunistic foreign competitors.

Most other corporations, however, are not so constrained. Du Pont, for example, appears to be joining the exodus from base businesses by acquiring major positions in biotechnology (New England Nuclear) and oil (Conoco). Monsanto asserted that having a health care business is a first priority and bought G.D. Searle. Other cash-rich or growth-obsessed firms continue to search for acquisitions. For a large firm like Ford, Philip Morris, or General Electric, the task is even more challenging; few target companies can add materially to the corporate revenues while satisfying any criteria for reasonable fit.

The results of all this mindful (or mindless) search for new opportunity have yet to be tabulated. But however realized, be it by internal development or by acquisition, diversification appears to be a risky strategy. The "conglomerate discount" applied by Wall Street in the 1970s to firms engaged in unrelated diversification reflected this reality. And indeed, the spate of leveraged buyouts and restructurings in the 1980s was fueled by the managerial recognition that the sum of the parts of many diversified corporations may be worth more than the whole.

Resource Acquisition

Once the corporation has decided how to allocate resources to each of the corporate opportunities, both internal and external, management must decide how to pay the bill. Resource allocation decisions are academic unless the appropriate investments can be made in support of these decisions. The financing decisions in effect address the question of whether the corporation can afford to pursue the strategies that have been selected. Although some investments may be only managerial, adequate and timely economic resources are often the major consideration.

In most corporations, unfortunately, the financing decisions are decoupled from the strategy decisions. The CEO will ratify the resource allocation decisions and the board of directors (at another meeting) will determine dividend policy or capital structure. This is a serious mistake, for strategy choices have financial consequences, and the relationships among growth rates, ROI, and other financial policies need to be clearly understood. For instance, decisions to incur more or less long-term debt have a profound effect on the firm's cost of capital and thus the threshold level of profitability for the firm's businesses. Decisions to pay out a greater or lesser amount of earnings in the form of dividends will change the amount of cash available for investment in support of business and corporate strategy.

An exhaustive discourse on corporate finance is beyond the scope of this book. We will at least address the effect of debt and dividends on financial performance, however, since both affect how rapidly the firm can increase earnings.

The relationship among these variables is best expressed by the following equation, sometimes referred to as the sustainable growth formula:

$$G = \frac{D}{E}(R-i)\,p + R\,p,$$

where G = growth in earnings
D = debt
E = equity
R = return on investment
i = cost of debt
p = dividend retention ratio

If the firm has no debt ($D = 0$), and all earnings are reinvested ($p = 1$), then earnings will grow at a rate equal to the return on investment ($G = R$). If the firm has no debt and all its earnings are paid out in the form of dividends, then $G = 0$, and the firm will not grow. Increasing debt increases growth, provided the interest rate is less than the rate of return. Higher debt also increases earnings per share but may reduce the price/earnings multiple if investors demand a premium to offset the higher variability of earnings over the business cycle. Excessive leverage is risky, since reductions in revenue imperil the interest coverage; the average debt-to-equity ratio for U.S. firms in 1986 was 0.46.

If new external funds are required, the options include various forms of debt and equity. Most corporate finance texts explain how to select a mix that minimizes the firm's cost of capital. The alternatives include internal financing versus external debt in its various forms, and dividend payout versus cash retention. A number of specific financial strategies merit mention.

Going Private.   Offsetting the surge in initial public offerings (IPOs) of new ventures during the past several years has been a growing trend for public firms to go private. Supporting this trend has been the increasing cost of satisfying the Securities and Exchange Commission's and other public reporting requirements (several hundred thousand dollars for most firms). The fantasy of greater riches for the present or potential owners may also be a factor.

Going private (defined by the SEC as a deregistration that reduces the number of stockholders to less than 300) can occur in several ways. The most publicized in recent years has been the leveraged buyout. This strategy has also become more attractive because of the greater availability of financing, often in the form of high-yield junk bonds. In this transaction, insiders, usually a group of senior managers, purchase the assets of the business for cash. The buyout is heavily leveraged with debt to be repaid from expected cash flow. The corporation can also effect a reverse stock split, exchange debentures for stock, repurchase stock, or merge with another private firm.

A variation on the theme of privatization is the strategy adopted by public firms to retain independence. Over 400 corporations have acted to protect their autonomy by adopting a variety of poison pill measures. Although the details of individual plans differ, the typical pill allows existing shareholders to purchase corporate stock at a discount after a hostile bidder has acquired a certain percentage of the company's equity. Some firms, regrettably, have also adopted the practice of greenmail, the payment of a premium over market value to acquire the stock of a hostile suitor.

Another strategy to ward off unwelcome suitors was introduced for the first time in 1982 after Bendix offered $43 a share for Martin Marietta stock with a market value of $33. Martin Marietta countered with a Pac Man defense, offering $75 a share for Bendix, then selling at $55. Allied ultimately intervened and bought Bendix, reselling Martin Marietta its own shares in exchange for Bendix stock. Burdened by heavy debt, Martin was forced to divest its cement, aluminum, and gravel businesses and now focuses on its high-technology aerospace and electronics businesses—the same strategy, ironically, that Bendix would have imposed.

A number of Pac Man defenses were later initiated by other firms, including Burlington Industries in a 1987 attempt to forestall a takeover by the Canadian multinational Dominion Textile (the Witch of the North). Burlington in the end resorted to a leveraged buyout in partnership with Morgan Stanley, a New York investment bank. A successful Pac Man defense was consummated in 1988 by American Brands. After E-II Holdings, a Beatrice spinoff, offered to acquire American Brands, their target responded with an attractive offer for E-II that prevailed.

Stock Repurchase.   Stock repurchase may be an appropriate strategy to adopt when stock price falls below a threshold level (presumed to be lower than the value of the corporation) or the corporation lacks more attractive opportunities to reinvest excess cash. The Coca-Cola Company recently adopted a plan to buy back more than 10 percent of the outstanding common stock over a three-year period at a cost of about $1.8 billion. The plan reflects corporate belief that the firm has insufficient debt in the capital structure—that it is underleveraged with only a 24 percent debt-to-equity ratio. If the plan were carried out, the debt ratio would rise to 35 percent, while dividend payout would remain at 40 percent of net earnings. Roberto Goizueta, Coca-Cola's chairman, has asserted that the program is "consistent with management's overriding object to create shareholder value."[25] Other corporations that committed to stock buyback in 1987 include American Express, General Motors, and Philip Morris.

Leveraged Recapitalization, Bankruptcy, and Liquidation.   The increase in merger and acquisition activity, particularly on the part of corporate raiders, has challenged corporate management to give renewed attention to shareholder value. The leveraged recapitalization has provided another response to this challenge. By substituting debt for the accumulated equity balances in the company, management accomplishes three objectives:

1. Protection from raiders by leveraging assets
2. Improved return on equity by greater financial leverage, and possible enhanced stock value
3. Increased management control

FMC Corporation, as an example, under pressure due to poor stock performance, recapitalized in 1986 by substituting $1.5 billion of additional debt for existing equity. Under the plan, shareholders received $80 in cash and one new share of the recapitalized company for every original share. Shareholders' equity was reduced from $1.12 billion to ($0.66) billion, while debt increased from $0.37 billion to $1.90 billion. As a result of the plan, employee and management ownership increased to 40 percent.

At Owens-Corning, by contrast, recapitalization was proposed in 1986 to thwart a potential takeover move by Wickes. The price of this defense was expected to include sale of assets, reduction of the work force, and reduced growth. According to William Boechenstein, Owens-Corning's chairman, "The plan is not painless. It also represents a major change in corporate strategy in that we will manage for cash flow rather than actively making major investments in potential future growth areas."[26]

Since its introduction by Multimedia in 1985, the leveraged recapitalization has been embraced by a host of firms, including Colt Industries, Allegis, and others. Most recapitalizations have performed well in the marketplace. But corporate performance under this strategy is very sensitive to interest rate fluctuations, and poor performance is magnified because of the heavy debt load (negative leverage may occur).

A radical form of financial strategy is represented by the retreat to Chapter XI bankruptcy. This ploy has been invoked in recent years by Johns-Manville, Penn Central, and Texaco as they seek protection from creditors or litigators. Selling all the assets of the firms and distributing the proceeds to the shareholders represents another example of an extreme financial strategy.

Relations with Stakeholders

The management of a firm's external relations can play an integral role in the successful implementation of strategy. This entails that the organization pay careful attention to the needs and demands (which often conflict with one another) of a variety of external stakeholders, including shareholders, the investment community, the board of directors, regulatory agencies, local and state governments, the community at large, and various special interest groups. Corporations must decide what posture they will adopt toward various stakeholders and must respond to the issues they raise. This requires a stance on business ethics, environmental coexistence, legal compliance, human rights, and a plethora of other considerations.

For example, noncompliance with the law is a policy apparently embraced by many firms, particularly regarding environmental statutes. After Hooker Chemical and Plastics Corporation was convicted in 1978 of polluting Florida's air with fluorides, documents revealed that corporate management knew and approved of the local violations. Lockheed's payoffs to foreign officials to secure aircraft orders, although not a violation of foreign business practices, raised serious questions about the company's practices in the United States.

Numerous defense contractors have now been convicted of knowingly bilking the government of millions through overbilling and as a result have been banned from bidding on new contracts. Although clearly a breach of ethical conduct, the practice appears commonplace. Revelations of speedometer fixing by Chrysler caused an uproar among American consumers and resulted in a public apology by Lee Iacocca in 1987.

Thus, the scandals resulting from accusations of price fixing, payoffs, and insider trading are forcing organizations to reevaluate their basic beliefs and ethical practice and develop policies on these issues before they become public relations problems. Few business schools now offer electives on business ethics, and still fewer have made them required.

A broader set of social issues dealing with corporate citizenship also are on the board docket. The heated debate over divestment in South Africa, the extent of Union Carbide's obligations for the Bhopal chemical disaster, the Johns-Manville liability for disability incurred by users of asbestos, and the question of who will bear the cost of nuclear power plant overruns—all are complex issues involving a myriad of stakeholders having divergent views.

Many corporations, like Johnson and Johnson in the wake of the Tylenol poisonings, have established crisis committees composed of key executives and specialists to respond to catastrophic events. Although these damage control groups have proved effective in coordinating resources and managing external communications, they are reactive rather than proactive. But the realities of today's society are forcing new postures to be assumed in advance of catastrophe. McDonald's recent decision to abandon the use of polyurethane containers because of fear that they contribute to the destruction of the earth's ozone layer, as one example, has earned them abundant goodwill with environmentalists.

Communications with the investment community remain an enormous opportunity for improvement on the part of most organizations. Few firms tell clear stories about their present and future strategies. As a result, investors are confused and disappointed when results do not appear to match the perceived strategy. The consequence for the firm is a devaluation in market price and increased vulnerability to corporate raiders.

The role of the board of directors has evolved dramatically in recent years. Although always charged with fiduciary responsibility on behalf of the stockholders, many early boards were passive—mere figureheads. But now boards are being held accountable for corporate performance; those who are derelict are now the object of litigation. One direct measure of this trend has been the increasing cost of directors' and officers' liability insurance. It is still the case, however, that the goals of managers and the goals of the board (representing the shareholders) may be divergent. As a result, a prudent corporation takes care to assure that the board participates in key policy decisions and also understands and endorses corporate strategy.

In the simplest case, it may be obvious that the other elements of corporate strategy are indeed responsive to stakeholders' needs. But more commonly, an audit will reveal varying degrees of current or potential malaise, and specific additional programs must be initiated.

SUMMARY

The logic for selecting corporate strategy begins, as in the case of business strategy formulation, with the establishing of an appropriate data base. After a number of alternative future scenarios are inspected, managers can commit to a specific set of strategies that are congruent with not only the available resources but also the values of the organization. The strategy entails continued application of the firm's distinctive competence or diversification. The perils of diversification are well documented. If the corporation cannot add value, that is, if it cannot derive some material benefit from shared resources or skills, it is better to let the shareholders manage their own portfolio of diversified investments.

Corporate strategy formulation represents the greatest opportunity for managerial creativity. It demands that managers be sensitive to the need for maximizing shareholders' value and achieving economic renewal by effective resource allocation. At the same time, it demands careful attention to managerial renewal and the advancement of corporate learning.

Good strategy sets the stage for economic and mangerial renewal. But good performance requires both effective strategy and good implementation, the topic to be discussed in Part III.

APPENDIX: THE MILLER CASE

In 1969 the Philip Morris Company, seeking opportunities to offset declining growth in its tobacco business, acquired 53 percent of the Miller Brewing Company from W.R. Grace for $130 million. The balance of the equity was bought in 1970 for $97 million. The total price amounted to a multiple of approximately 25 times earnings, and the price exceeded book value by about $150 million. John Murphy, a veteran of Philip Morris's tobacco wars, was given the mandate to apply the corporation's marketing expertise to the revitalization of Miller.

Murphy succeeded brilliantly in implementing a strategy that catapulted Miller from a weak number 7 in the industry in 1970 to a strong number 2 in 1984 (Table 5–A1). Prior to 1970 the name of the game was distribution. Regional brewers held strong market positions in many sectors of the country, a legacy of the days before refrigerated tank cars were available to support brewers' aspirations toward national distribution. Miller changed the basis of competition to advertising and

Table 5–A1.   Market Share for the Miller Brewing Company.

Year	Miller Share (%)	Miller Rank	Anheuser-Busch Share (%)	Anheuser-Busch Rank
1970	4.2	7	18.2	1
1971	4.0	7	18.9	1
1972	4.0	7	18.7	1
1973	5.0	5	19.1	1
1974	6.2	5	23.4	1
1975	8.7	4	23.7	1
1976	12.1	3	19.3	1
1977	15.4	2	23.3	1
1978	19.3	2	25.6	1
1979	20.7	2	26.7	1
1980	21.5	2	28.9	1
1981	22.8	2	30.8	1
1982	22.3	2	33.5	1
1983	21.1	2	34.1	1
1984	20.5	2	34.0	1

promotion, supporting this new approach with marketing expenditures that soared from $12 million in 1970 to $165 million in 1984.

The leader, Anheuser-Busch, kept pace. Indeed, except for a loss in share in 1976 when a strike reduced production capacity, Anheuser-Busch matched Miller's growth in every year. The losers were the smaller competitors who were unable to expend the advertising dollars necessary to play with the leaders; economies of scale gave Miller and Busch a large advantage in advertising cost per barrel. As a result, many of the small regionals succumbed to cost/price squeeze and either stopped operations or were acquired. Schlitz (number 2), Pabst (number 3), and Schaefer (number 5) were all gone by 1980.

The Miller strategy was successful. But was the game worth the candle? Operating profit for Miller (Figure 5–A1) increased from $11 million in 1970 to $227 million in 1983, a handsome increase and a better return on sales than when the game began. But the net assets of $167 million in 1970 had also increased proportionately. Capital expenditures during this period exceeded $1.5 billion, and cash flow was negative from 1971 to 1981! On a discounted cash flow basis, the internal rate of return (IRR) of the strategy from 1970 to 1984 was a mere 3.6 percent, even assuming a terminal value of nine times 1984 earnings. Thus, the economic return was low—far less than any reasonable hurdle rate.

Figure 5–A1. Miller Operating Statistics.

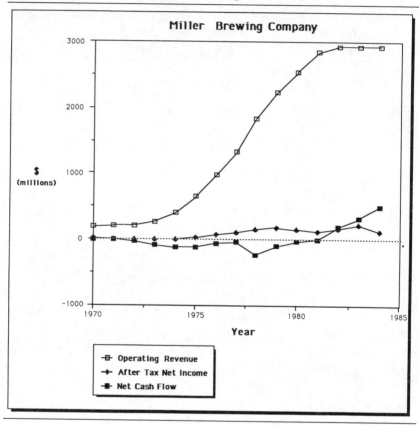

Could the corporation have found better use for the invested funds? Even the shareholders would have realized greater return from investment in grade A corporate bonds. But the dilemma faced by Philip Morris is not extraordinary. Most managers, when faced with reduced growth and increased cash flow, feel obligated to spend it, ostensibly to assure economic renewal. A strategy of diversification is the usual response, and discounted cash flow projections are often ignored or are inaccurate because of the firm's ignorance of an unfamiliar industry.

NOTES

1.   Although in the United States, government regulation has crippled the nuclear power industry (no new order has been placed since 1978). France, by contrast, now derives 70 percent of its energy output from nuclear energy.

2.   The alligator and some other mammals possess a third eyelid (the nictitating membrane). While this eyelid protects them, it also prevents them from seeing—like managers who think they have no choices.

3.   John A. Byrne, "Culture Shock at Xerox," *Business Week*, June 22, 1987.

4.   Thomas S. Kuhn's work on paradigm shifts in science is relevant to this injunction. See Kuhn's *The Structure of Scientific Revolutions* (Chicago: The University of Chicago Press, 1970).

5.   Arthur Koestler, *The Yogi and The Commissar* (New York: The MacMillan Company, 1965).

6.   Herman Kahn and Anthony J. Wiener, *The Year 2000*, (New York: MacMillan, 1967).

7.   Dennis Meadows et al., *The Limits to Growth* (New York: Universe Books, 1972); E. Pestel and M. Mesarovic, *Mankind at the Turning Point* (New York: Dutton, 1974).

8.   Pierre Wack, "Scenarios: Uncharted Waters Ahead," *Harvard Business Review* (September–October 1985).

9.   Hall (*Management Science, 30*, no. 8, August 1984) invokes an interesting origami metaphor. In origami (Japanese paper-folding), the order of paper folds determines the object to be created; once a fold is made, only certain objects are possible. In a similar manner, a company's future becomes enfolded by the order of management response to critical events.

10. Robert J. Allio, "Forecasting: The Myth of Control," *Planning Review* (May 1986).

11. A recent parallel to this concept has been the Kepner-Tregoe notion of *driving force*, a term developed to characterize the primary strategic orientation of the firm. The nine possible driving forces include products (Ford), market needs (Playboy), technology (Cray), production (U.S. Steel), method of sale (Avon), method of distribution (Canteen Service), natural resources (DeBeers), size-growth (Litton), and return on investment or profit (ITT). The one-dimensional quality of the driving force concept, however, may lead executives to dangerously simplistic strategy choices. See Charles H. Kepner and Benjamin Tregoe, *The Rational Manager* (Princeton, NJ: Princeton Research Pr., 1976).

12. Russell L. Ackoff expands on this theme in his *Management in Small Doses* (New York: John Wiley & Sons, Inc., 1986).

13. Michael Hergert, "Strategic Resource Allocation Using Divisional Hurdle Rates," *Planning Review* (January–February 1987).

14.   Although excess diversity may impair financial performance, moving the entire corporation from one industry to another represents a special case of diversification that may have beneficial results (viz Jerry Tsai's transformation of American Can).

15.   Richard P. Rumelt, "Strategy, Structure, and Economic Performance," Division of Research, Harvard University, 1974.

16.   The theory of unrelated or conglomerate diversification, pioneered by ITT, Textron, and others, is to maximize overall corporate performance by adding or divesting businesses that can add value, regardless of their product or market relatedness.

17.   H. Kurt Christensen and C.A. Montgomery, "Corporate Economic Performance," *Strategic Management Journal*, no. 2. (1981); Richard A. Bettis and Vijay Mahajan, "Risk/Return Performance of Diversified Firms," *Management Science, 31*, no. 7 (July 1985).

18.   Ralph Biggadike, "The Risky Business of Diversification," *Harvard Business Review* (May–June 1979).

19.   Kenneth Davidson, "Do Megamergers Make Sense?" *Journal of Business Strategy* (Winter 1987).

20.   F.M. Scherer, *Journal of Economic Perspectives, 2*, no. 1, (Winter 1988).

21.   Walter Adams and James W. Brock, "The Hidden Costs of Failed Mergers," *The New York Times*, June 21, 1987, p. 3.

22.   W.T. Grimm, *Mergerstat Review*, 1986.

23.   Paul E. Lego, Remarks at 1987 Security Analysts meeting, New York, March 27, 1987.

24.   R. Glenn Souza, "Shopping for a Company?" Financial Executives Institute, Morristown, NJ, 1986.

25.   Jonathan P. Hicks, "Coke Plans Buyback of Shares," *The New York Times*, July 20, 1987, p. 35.

26.   John J. Keller, "Owens-Corning Saves Itself—With a Scorched-Earth Strategy," *Business Week*, September 15, 1986, p. 49.

6 FORMULATING GLOBAL STRATEGY

Global competition, unlike searches for excellence and one-minute management, is more than this year's fad. Since the turn of the century, corporations have struggled with the complexities of managing international or multinational businesses.

Global competition has already permeated many industries. A strong indicator is the changing lineup of competitors for U.S. companies. GM and Ford now go head-to-head in automobiles with Toyota, Daimler Benz, and Hyundai. General Electric and Westinghouse now battle Siemens and Mitsubishi in power generation equipment. Caterpillar and Deere take on Komatsu instead of Harvester in the construction equipment industry. Goodyear competes with Michelin, Bridgestone, and Pirelli. Boeing and McDonnell Douglas fight it out with Airbus. U.S. textile firms face off against Brazil and Portugal.

The list of industries that experience global competition (soft drinks, vitamins, cosmetics, photographic film, semiconductors, computers, shipbuilding, motorcycles, watches are other examples) is getting longer. The list of domestic industries (furniture, printing, retailing, consumer packaged goods, retail banking), on the other hand, is dwindling. Even in these industries, many products and components are purchased offshore.

For many firms the maturity of local markets has induced them to seek growth abroad, where they face counterparts from other countries, as well as new types of competitors, and governments that play an increasing role in determining how the game is to be played in local markets. The spread of global competition has been driven by the growing similarity of many markets around the world and the homogenization of demand. Advertising and promotion have accelerated these trends. The reduction in trade and tariff barriers has also facilitated broad distribution of standardized goods and services across national boundaries, as has increased mobility of capital.

Competitors who are alert to global opportunities can take advantage of economies of scale in R&D, manufacturing, marketing, and distribution, and purchasing to an extent not possible in domestic markets alone. Technology has also been a driving force: it has destabilized many competitive arenas, creating opportunities for both new and existing competitors and permitting firms to tailor products to the needs and idiosyncrasies of local markets. The restructuring of banking and the many new entrants in telecommunications and electronics highlight these trends.

The insidious displacement of shortsighted players in a global industry is no better illustrated than by the retrospective list of U.S. television manufacturers. The 27 U.S. producers in 1960 have now dwindled to a list of only five U.S. survivors, plus seven Japanese and South Korean manufacturers.[1]

THE RCA SAGA

The demise of RCA in the color television industry is instructive. The major contibutor to the development of color TV, RCA realized its first sales in 1954, although market acceptance was slow. As a result RCA did not make a profit until the early 1960s. But by 1969 the Japanese had taken over.

The first element of Japanese penetration into the U.S. market entailed private label sales using U.S. brands and distribution networks. The low Japanese costs enabled them to provide high profit margins to dealers while offering low prices to the consumer. The 1964 contract between Toshiba and Sears exemplified this arrangement. The long-term result was a domination by the Japanese of low-cost distribution channels; private label sales increased to over 20 percent of the U.S. total by 1970.

This shift in distribution was facilitated by the high reliability of Japanese products, which reduced the need for trained service staff and service centers. GE, among others, disparaged the Japanese as being unable to overcome this apparent handicap, particularly since GE prided itself on having an extensive network of local sales and service centers. Japanese products also filled the market void in small-screen sets, as U.S. firms had emphasized high-margin, large-screen sets.

Technology was also a key factor in RCA's downfall. Although RCA was the innovator, they graciously shared their technology by licenses, rather than using their technology as the basis for entry to overseas markets. Sony and Matsushita applied and built upon the U.S. technology. Sony introduced the Trinitron in 1968 and the Japanese in general successfully applied integrated circuitry to the production of reliable compact sets. The Japanese strategy in Europe was a replica of the U.S. strategy and was equally successful.

Investments in the United States by foreign firms continue to accelerate, giving them a better foothold from which to attack entrenched U.S. firms. Shifts in ownership have been facilitated by recent declines in the market value of U.S. firms, although the statistics on the export performance of domestically based U.S. operations show more aggressive performance than is sometimes alleged by the press. U.S. trade performance indeed deteriorated dramatically between 1957 and 1983. But if the overall export performance of U.S. corporations, including shipments from overseas operations, is computed, a more favorable picture emerges: share of world manufacturing exports between 1966 and 1983 has been virtually constant at 17.7 percent.[2]

RECOGNIZING A GLOBAL INDUSTRY

What is the essential difference between businesses that demand global strategies and those that can continue to compete only on a domestic basis? Global competitors exploit the similarities among countries to enhance competitive advantage, whereas multidomestic (or multinational) competitors exploit the differences among countries. In multidomestic industries, competition in one market occurs independently of competition elsewhere and competing internationally is optional. In other words the set of multinational businesses (in publishing, for example) can be managed as a portfolio, whereas a global business must be managed with a single integrated strategy, even if it serves different markets.

In global industries a firm's competitive position in one market or country may be strengthened (or weakened) by its position in other markets, and is a function of its ability to capitalize on intracompany linkages and economics of scale in sourcing, distribution, product development, and the like. This is in dramatic contrast to a portfolio approach to a corporation's businesses.

Competitors in global industries serve common customer needs with standardized products or services that satisfy global quality standards. The resultant scale economies in technology, marketing, or production often create substantial entry barriers. In a multidomestic industry, on the other hand, heterogeneous markets demand different products. High transportation costs may discourage cross-border shipping. Products are often distributed through local channels, and local customers may demand quick service or short lead times. As a consequence, the market is often served most efficiently by a diverse set of local competitors who do not experience significant economies of scale.

Global strategy may be implemented differently in different product-market segments. For example, the markets served by the motorcycle industry—a true global industry—can be split into three discrete segments. In the less-developed countries, the motorcycle represents a primary mode of transportation. In the United States, the motorcycle is primarily a recreational vehicle. In Europe the function of the motorcycle is in transition as cars replace them for basic transportation. Successful competitors like Honda serve all three markets.

Ohmae stresses the emerging importance of the triad markets (North America, Western Europe, and Japan). These three markets constitute a single collection of 630 million consumers having some common needs. In Ohmae's view, global competitors must play in each of the triad markets in order to serve the strategic developing markets.

THE POLITICAL DIMENSION

In the next decade the greatest challenge for many U.S. managers will be how to succeed against foreign competitors. Even the U.S. Congress has singled out competitiveness as America's "dominant economic issue" for the balance of the twentieth century. Industrial policy panaceas that provide support for emerging or faltering industries are no longer in favor; a new spectrum of nostrums is being offered by Democrats and Republicans alike. These include changes in trade legislation, reduction in budget deficits, and incentives to promote business and government collaboration. To the manager beleaguered by low-cost imports, these prescriptions may be reassuring, but immediate relief is unlikely to come from any government initiatives.

In the long term, U.S. firms will benefit enormously from a more pragmatic approach to dealing with the policies adopted by foreign economic systems. The current system of the General Agreement on Tariffs and Trade (GATT) addresses 80 percent of world trade through a complex process of multilateral negotiation. But economic systems dedicated to free trade and open markets represent a mere 27 percent of world trade.[3] Other systems, including centrally planned economies (the USSR), developing economies (the Third World), mixed economies (France), and plan-driven systems (Japan and South Korea) constitute the balance. Protectionism is surely not the answer. A more realistic negotiating approach, exemplified perhaps by the recent U.S.-Canada bilateral agreement, is required.

Although effective global strategy must recognize the vagaries of government policy, the ultimate answer is to be responsive to market needs and competitive forces. The turnaround achieved by Harley-Davidson illustrates this principle.[4] Although founded in 1903, by 1983 Harley hovered on the brink of extinction as the last U.S. motorcycle manufacturer, despite the imposition of heavy tariffs on imported large motorcycles. Harley-Davidson was taken public in 1965 and was subsequently bought by AMF. But in 1981, frustrated by their inability to convince the corporation that their proposed strategy would be effective, a group of managers executed a leveraged buyout. Since that time, major improvements in quality, cost, and inventory control, complemented by a decentralization of decision making, have returned the firm to profitability. In fact, Harley's competitive position has improved so dramatically that in 1985 management asked the Reagan administration to remove tariff protection.

Other competitors in the motorcycle industry waited too long. In its dying moments, the British motorcycle industry was producing motorcycles at the rate of 18 per man-year, while the Japanese were already turning them out at the rate of 200–350 per man-year. The Japanese advantage proved insurmountable.

GLOBAL STRATEGY MODELS

Global strategy becomes critical when the need for local adaption is low and benefits from global systems are high, either as a result of economies of scale or economies of scope. Some examples of scope economies are shown in Table 6-1. (The notion of sharing investment across the value chain for different product-market segments was addressed in the discussion of field theory in Chapter 3.) Conversely,

Table 6–1. Scope Economies in Product and Market Diversification.

	Sources of Scope Economies	
	Product Diversification	*Market Diversification*
Shared physical assets	Factory automation with flexibility to produce multiple products	Global brand name
	(Ford)	(Coca-Cola)
Shared external relations	Using common distribution channel for multiple products	Servicing multinational customers worldwide
	(Matsushita)	(Citibank)
Shared learning	Sharing R&D in computer and communications businesses	Pooling knowledge developed in different markets
	(NEC)	(Procter & Gamble)

Source: Sumantra Ghosal, "Global Strategy: An Organizing Framework," *Strategic Management Journal* (September–October 1987). Copyright © 1987. Reprinted by permission of John Wiley & Sons, Ltd.

industries can remain national when local needs are unique (a premium is placed on responsiveness to the customer) and few economies of scale can be identified. Some industries, like telecommunications, may be considered "blocked global"—impeded in their evolution by government policies.[5]

Michael Porter's system is similar, dividing effective strategies into four broad categories:[6]

Global Cost Leadership or Differentiation.   Global cost leaders, such as Toyota or Komatsu, sell standardized products and benefit from economies of scale. Global differentiators seek competitive advantage on the basis of unique quality or features. IBM, for example, offers global customers the benefits of a broad product line, extensive software support, and a global service network.

Global Segmentation.   Smaller firms may elect to serve one or a few industry segments on a worldwide basis. Mercedes in automobiles exemplifies this strategy, with its concentration on the luxury upscale market.

Protected Markets.   This strategy entails serving markets that are protected by host governments. Opportunities to exploit this strategy are most often found in developing countries, although in some industries even developed countries offer incentives. Volkswagen's strategy in Brazil is an example of this approach; its arrangement with the government gives VW a preferred position in manufacturing to serve local markets, although in 1986 they lost money.

National Responsiveness.   Competitors executing this strategy seek to meet the unique needs of local markets, thus sacrificing some of the cost advantages of a pure global strategy. (In its extreme form, this is the strategy adopted by the multidomestic competitor).

SEVEN PRESCRIPTIONS FOR WINNING GLOBALLY

There are no facile prescriptions for winning global battles. For the business confronted by global competition, the practical strategist invokes seven guidelines for winning:

Get to new global markets first.   It's devilishly hard to overtake the first players in any market. The history of small cars in North America (introduced originally by Volkswagen and the Japanese) is a classic illustration of this maxim. Achieving market share in the latter stages of market development is a lost cause for most businesses.

Entry to foreign markets is often facilitated by joint ventures with local investors (including the government). Allowing local partners to retain substantial equity in the enterprise can yield substantial advantage over other global competitors.

Counterattack at home.   Global competitors often fund growth in new overseas markets from the profits in their own domestic markets. Competitor cash flow can be interrupted by attacking them at home. Recent illustrations of this tactic include the 3M attack on Japanese markets for memory media (audiotape and videotape), and the Kodak assault on Fuji's domestic market for color photographic film after Fuji had succeeded in capturing 8 percent of Kodak's U.S. market. The technique of cross-subsidization has been an effective weapon in other industries, including tires and television.[7]

A provocative mirror strategy has been adopted by Honda. Struggling in a number 3 position in its domestic markets behind Toyota and Nissan, it has concentrated on export markets. Thus, the Honda strategy for automobiles has been to build profitable overseas business before conquering domestic competitors.

Invest in new technology.   Technology is a powerful ally in the global game, particularly if it enables a business to improve its cost position or product offering or to process information more efficiently. Losers hang on to old technology in the mistaken belief that incremental improvements can forestall the effect of a technological breakthrough. The continuing investment by U.S. Steel in old open hearth technology in the 1950s opened the door for Japanese competitors willing to commit to new basic oxygen technology and continuous casting.

Although the payoff for those firms willing to invest in technology is invariably higher productivity, many firms fail to consider the linked effects of productivity and exchange rates, not a factor under the old Bretton Woods system. Current floating exchange rate mechanisms require, in the absence of tariffs or other protectionist measures, that a company must be at least as productive relative to its own national economy as its international competitor is to its national economy.[8] Thus, if a business is situated in an inefficient country, greater productivity than the average firm is the key. Firms who fail to meet this requirement may find their absolute productivity advantages eroded through exchange rate or wage adjustments.

Consider alternative sourcing.   Productivity improvements to be derived from capital investments in new automated facilities may not be great enough to overcome the handicap of high labor costs. And investing in overseas production facilities may bring other benefits. Dominion Textile, Canada's leading textile manufacturer, as one example, established a denim manufacturing facility in Tunisia that not only provided a cost advantage but also gave access to the European Common Market.

Even the automobile firms are moving to reduce their vertical integration. By sourcing an increasing fraction of their parts requirements outside the corporation, they are realizing the benefits of lower labor cost. The Japanese competitors are only 25 percent integrated, as compared with 70 percent for General Motors, 50 percent for Ford, and 30 percent for Chrysler.

Install the right managerial system.   Assign managers to global businesses who understand the nuances of implementing global strategy in a local market. Losers rely on standardized organization structures and reward systems or allow local baronies to dictate how the game will be played. The 3M global planning system, as one example, integrates operations in 44 countries under the umbrella of a set of 19 business unit plans. Performance of country managers is measured primarily by their contribution to the success of each of the 19 global businesses.

Take early losses if necessary.   To sustain a global plan, competitors must be willing to sacrifice short-term profit for long-term rewards. Thus, a sacrifice in quarter-to-quarter performance in a global business may be the necessary price for long-term success. This may mean a system of variable hurdle rates that recognize either intrinsic differences in the cost of capital or the effect of market maturity on profitability. In a global strategy, in other words, losses can be expected (and must be tolerated) in emerging markets. The Japanese, for example, are reputed to have lost money for seven years during their assault on the European motorcycle market.

All of these guidelines will resonate with the classic strategic principles for winning domestically. The last principle, however, may clash with managerial illusions of American supremacy or Emersonian self-reliance, although it may well be the most important.

Join forces with competitors.   As any industry matures, be it domestic or global, the number of viable competitors invariably dwindles. And in global competition, an important pattern can be discerned: Low-cost competitors from less-developed countries have a disagreeable tendency to displace early leaders in developed countries, regardless of leaders' dedication to improved productivity. Consumer electronics, shipbuilding, motorcycles, and automobiles are good illustrations of this phenomenon. The global steel industry (Table 6–2) provides a dramatic stereotype: U.S. firms overtaken initially by Japan with its combination of low labor costs and contemporary technology, and Japan later falling victim to the equally aggressive South Koreans.

The solution is to plan early on to collaborate with other players who have competitive advantage in another part of the value chain, be it development, production, marketing, or finance. Partners who align early form the happiest marriages. Latecomers find that two losers

Table 6–2.   Steel Production, 1984 Labor Costs.

	Labor Productivity (hours/tonne)	Hourly Compensation $U.S.	Labor Cost ($U.S./tonne)
South Korea	4.02	2.16	8.64
EEC	5.45	10.38	56.27
Japan	5.98	11.12	66.50
United States	7.10	20.24	143.70

Source: Chase Econometrics.

don't make a winner. Alliances at the national level are best illustrated by Airbus, a consortium of Europe's leading civil aircraft manufacturers, including Aerospatiale (France), Bolkow-Blohm GmbH (West Germany), British Aerospace PLC (UK), and Construcciones Aeronauticas SA (Spain). An estimated $10 billion in funding from the sponsors has enabled Airbus to move into second place in the industry behind Boeing, the world leader with 60 percent of the market.

Chrysler's recent deals with both American Motors and Mitsubishi exemplify this strategy, as does the recently formed coalition of U.S. semiconductor manufacturers to produce advanced technology chips. And the AT&T linkup with Olivetti, the Italian computer maker, is yet another example of the trend toward strategic alliances and away from multinationals.

In the final analysis, selecting an effective global strategy is no different from selecting a strategy for any business. The playing field may be larger, and cultural differences or political forces may increase complexity, and the risks may be greater. But the successful global player still differentiates itself from the competition in a way that the customer values.

NOTES

1. In July 1987 GE sold its GE and RCA brands to Thomson, the French consumer electronics firm, leaving Zenith as the only major U.S. manufacturer.
2. Robert E. Lipsey and Irving B. Kravis, "Business Holds Its Own as America Slips," *The New York Times*, January 18, 1987, p. 22.
3. Pat Choate and Juyne Linger, "Tailored Trade: Dealing with the World as It Is" *Harvard Business Review*, January–February 1988, p. 91.
4. Nicholas D. Kristof, "Harley-Davidson Roars Back," *The New York Times*, October 3, 1985, p. 1.
5. Herbert Henzler and Wilhelm Rall, "Facing Up to the Globalization Challenge," *The McKinsey Quarterly*, Winter 1986, p. 56.
6. Michael E. Porter, in *Competition in Global Industries* (Boston: Harvard Business School Press, 1987).
7. Gary Hamel and C.K. Prahalad, "Do You Really Have a Global Strategy?," *Harvard Business Review* (July–August 1985).
8. M.C. Bogue and E.S. Buffa, *Corporate Strategic Analysis* (New York: Macmillan, 1986).

III IMPLEMENTING STRATEGY AND MEASURING PERFORMANCE

Once strategies have been formulated, they must be effectively implemented to realize any change in business or corporate performance. Assuming that leadership has secured commitment from the organization, managers must be assigned accountability for each strategy, and progress must be monitored using relevant measures of performance.

The role of managerial systems is crucial to the implementation process. Is the corporate organization structure consonant with its strategy? Will corporate decisions be centralized or decentralized (and to what degree)? Participative or autocratic? What information is needed to make good decisions? These managerial system decisions are crucial. Congruent and differentiated systems facilitate strategy implementation, while inappropriate systems impede strategy implementation or cause strategy to fail.

Finally we must deal with the measurement of performance. At the level of both the business and the corportion, relevant financial and strategic measures are needed. Thus, in Part III we address the final stage of practical strategy—the steps necessary to assure that good strategy produces good results.

7 IMPLEMENTATION

Eloquent statements of strategy have little value if they are not implemented. Managers need to put in place the programs necessary to assure timely implementation, and they must clearly define responsibility and accountability for each major program. Labor, equipment, cash, and other resources are applied to these corporate or business programs. The essential requirement is that programs in all functional areas be driven by business or corporate strategy. Too often, unfortunately, managers attempt to rationalize strategy on the basis of programs that have already been developed. A process for assuring that strategy is linked to action programs would include the following steps:

1. Identify the strategy.
2. Describe the dimensions of the strategy.
   - Specific product and market segments to which it will apply
   - Time frame for the strategy
   - Competitors the strategy will affect
   - Expected results
3. Identify the strengths or weaknesses the strategy builds on or corrects.
4. Describe the probable competitor response to the strategy.
5. Identify the specific programs required to implement the strategy.
6. Designate the function, organizational unit, or individual responsible for the strategy.

7. Present a schedule of incremental investment and expense by year required to implement the programs.
8. List the key parameters to be monitored as the strategy is carried out.
9. Identify the critical issues that relate to the strategy.

Assuming that adequate resources are allocated to carrying out strategy, the key to successful implementation is the *managerial systems* of the corporation. Managerial systems include:

*   Organization design and structure
*   Information and decision systems
*   Planning systems
*   Measurement and control systems
*   Management selection and development
*   Reward systems

The managerial systems describe the policies, procedures, and mechanisms through which strategy and programs are carried out. For example, the organization of the corporation determines the roles to be played by individuals or organizational units. The measurement and control system specifies the parameters to be monitored as strategy is being implemented, and how much variance from plan can be tolerated. The reward system reflects the performance expectations of the firm and motivates managers to strive to achieve appropriate goals. Thus, the managerial systems comprise the infrastructure of the corporation, the fabric that supports managerial initiative. These systems must be designed to support corporate and business strategy.

ORGANIZATION DESIGN AND STRUCTURE

Organizational design usually first addresses issues of legal form. Should the corporation, for example, be private or public? Public firms have access to greater sources of equity capital and can increase the firm's liquidity. Private firms, on the other hand, shield themselves from the market's pressure for short-term earnings and perhaps enhance their ability to manage strategically.

Strategy implementation requires that we go beyond the legal formalities to consider all the classic issues of organization structure. A decentralized organization maximizes flexibility in responding to market needs. A centralized organization minimizes duplication and perhaps cost. Recent empirical data, moreover, appear to show that a decentralized organization of autonomous businesses tends to enhance sales growth, whereas a centralized organization generates higher return on investment.[1]

A functional organization makes sense when a firm is offering one product or service to a single market. But when products or markets proliferate, a profit center or divisional organization is often more reasonable.[2] GE's centralized organization with six functions endured from 1878 to 1955 before giving way to a decentralized departmental organization. Diversity, thus, appears to foster decentralization (although the irony is that decentralization tends to promote diversity).

A matrix organization is sometimes selected as the solution to the need for sharing resources. But an organization that assigns responsibilities for product and market to different managers, for example, will be difficult to manage, for ambiguities in authority often create uncomfortable managerial conflicts. If these ambiguities can be tolerated, of course, the matrix brings conflicting concerns into focus at the lowest level of the organization having expertise to make decisions.

Structure should follow strategy, that is, be aligned to support the business strategies of the firm.[3] But strategy tends to follow structure (yet another irony). Examples of this correlation were apparent in the computer industry in the 1970s, when IBM's monolithic centralized organization produced a line of main frame (monolithic) computers. At Digital Equipment, on the other hand, the natural product to emerge from DEC's highly decentralized organization was a set of distributed data processing devices—in particular the minicomputer. IBM's 1988 reorganization represents an attempt to coordinate its organization with the strategy necessary to serve the increasing number of computer market segments.

As another example of the effect of structure on strategy, consider the R&D laboratory that reports to the head of the manufacturing function; its natural focus will be on production efficiency. Conversely, the R&D laboratory that reports to the head of the marketing function will typically assign first priority to new product development.

Establishing responsibility and accountability for profit and cost (a cardinal principle of organization design) is best accomplished when the corporation organizes by business. Profit center organizations tend to focus on short-term performance. Product, market, or functional organizations suffer similar deficiencies and yield suboptimal performance. They also make it difficult to observe another essential principle of practical strategy—always allocate resources to corporate or business strategies.

INFORMATION AND DECISION SYSTEMS

The design of an organization creates a structure, but action by the decisions made by an organization are no better than the quality of the data feeding the decision-making process. And the quality of data can dramatically affect implementation (Is the project within schedule and budget?) as well as strategy (Which products are more profitable?).

Data are invariably abundant, but both individuals and corporations have a perceptual bandwidth that can accommodate only so much information (approximately seven bits of data at a time). These data absorption limits usually produce a condition known as "bounded rationality." The challenge, therefore, is to identify those data that are relevant and important and quickly screen out irrelevant data.[4] The necessary elements of a business and corporate data base are discussed in Chapters 3 and 7.

Having the right data is not enough. Equally important is the system by which organizations process data to reach decisions. Organizations always make decisions (respond to data) in a way that appears to maximize their own utility, that is, the expected value of the results. Our dilemma, unfortunately, is that the contents of any utility model are usually hidden, although often they can be inferred from the behavior of the organization. Furthermore, decision making for the firm is invariably nonrational; that is, the firm rarely acts in a way that maximizes its economic utility function. The "rationality" of decisions may be distorted by the need to maintain the health of the organization and avoid threats to its stability or by the needs of managers to satisfy their personal goals. Negotiations around political goals, furthermore, typically tend to produce decisions that satisfice (are good enough) rather that optimize (do as well as possible). Managers should not be surprised, therefore, that most decisions are a blend of rationality and nonrationality.

One useful set of paradigms for decision making include the *rational actor, organizational process,* and *bureaucratic politics* models.[5] In the rational actor model, rational decisions are made to optimize the performance of the entire system. In the organizational process model, decisions are the natural result of a set of well-established organizational systems and procedures. In the bureaucratic politics situation, decisions are the result of political bargaining among individuals and groups.

Examples of the organizational process model include the Apollo project (the need for NASA and its sister departments to identify a mission justifying their existence) and the decisions taken by OPEC and the Seven Sisters in perpetuating an oil cartel. The bureaucratic politics model is exemplified by the reluctance of successive U.S. presidents to withdraw from Vietnam. Many business organizations favor a well-defined hierarchical decision process. But in other organizations (like universities), the authority to make decisions is broadly dispersed among many stakeholders, and the governance process sacrifices efficiency in decision making in an effort to satisfy many stakeholders. In fact, the attempt by some corporations in the 1970s and 1980s to maximize participation in decision making has often been used to rationalize the abdication of leadership.[6]

The practical strategist understands the subtleties of decision making in the organization, be it power oriented (dominated by a personality or coalition), role oriented (emphasizing roles or hierarchical position), or task oriented (emphasizing task achievement).

PLANNING SYSTEMS

The history of planning in the modern corporation is short, spanning perhaps only a 100-year period (although planning in military organizations dates from the time of the Greek city-state). During the early days of the industrial revolution, planning was simply an expression of the intuition of the owner-manager, his personal strategic vision. Since early businesses were neither large nor complex, this *entrepreneurial* approach to planning proved to be perfectly adequate.

Formal long-range planning had its genesis in the 1920s in large corporations such as Du Pont and General Motors. Market demands for higher output led management to emphasize efficiency, yield, and throughput. As a result, early planning focused on the manufacturing function. Long-range capital plans, R&D plans, and ultimately marketing plans followed. This represented the era of the *functional long-range plan*.

The availability of plans for each of the functions of the organization inevitably led to the demand for integration. As a consequence, in the early 1950s we witnessed the first *comprehensive business plan*. Such a plan is produced by assembling plans for each of the functions of the organization into a single document. A financial consolidation is prepared by the controller, and the embellishment of an executive summary is added. The customary measures of performance are short-term profit and sales growth, applied uniformly to all divisions of the corporation.

Most U.S. corporations had adopted a comprehensive business planning process by the early 1970s, and this system is still utilized by a significant number of firms. But by the mid-1970s, a number of new phenomena were noted:

- *Reduced growth.* Historic rates of growth waned in many industries.
- *Greater competition.* New foreign competitors added to the already intense domestic competition for market share, particularly in mature industries such as automobiles and steel (the "smokestack" industries).
- *Declining profitability.* Despite the increased number of professional managers now populating the North American corporate world, performance was sluggish. Higher efficiency no longer seemed to be enough to offset the inroads of aggressive competitors. Many firms diversified to maintain the growth patterns of the 1960s, thus exacerbating managerial difficulties.
- *Higher uncertainty.* Although managers gave increased attention to sophisticated forecasting methodologies, the reliability of long-range forecasts declined. Discontinuities in the external environment, such as the oil embargo in 1973, added to their discomfort.

Thus, the stage was set for an era characterized by the preparation of *strategic plans*. Managerial attention shifted from the organizational unit, profit center, or functional department to the business itself as the legitimate beneficiary for resource allocation. A clear distinction began to emerge among business strategy, corporate strategy, operating strategy. As distinguished from the comprehensive business plan, the strategic plan stressed external competition by the business. Managers began to assign different standards of performance to different businesses, and the criteria shifted from return on sales (profit) to return on investment (asset utilization) as the increasing cost of capital highlighted the need for better resource management. New planning technologies were introduced to help managers make better resource allocation decisions, and the art of planning began to move toward a science in which certain strategies in a particular situation could be predicted to have specific outcomes.

In a well-designed planning system, the time horizon, frequency, and format will be carefully specified.

Time Horizon

Selecting the proper time horizon for planning is important. Plans that specify strategy and performance for many years have little credibility. On the other hand, a planning horizon that is too short invariably exaggerates the importance of short-term profit, and few investments are made to secure the long-term viability of the firm. The right planning horizon is neither too short nor too long. For most businesses, I favor a three-year period. Shorter intervals tend to result in harvesting, premature withdrawal from the industry. Longer intervals require clairvoyance about the future, although in some industries (forest products, distilled spirits, electric power generation), the long production or manufacturing cycle demands a long time horizon. And the planning horizon for *corporations* can be limited only by the imagination of the management.[7]

Frequency

How often should a formal plan be prepared or updated? Most corporations adopt an annual cycle of formal planning because plans can then be segued into the annual budgets (another ritual that needs reappraisal). But strategy should be revised whenever the assumptions on which the strategy was based change materially—that is, whenever the industry, market conditions, or competitive climate change. In venerable and stable industries, revisions may need to occur only every three or four years. In volatile industries like computer software or toys, strategies need more frequent revision.

Format

The proper format for a strategic plan allows the essential information to be conveyed to the interested parties—those who have a need to know, including senior executives and fellow managers. This entails that the plan focus on information that is relevant and filter out data that are not. The governing principle, then, is one of parsimony. The curse of the planning process is the three-pound plan. It connotes a failure to grasp the essence of the business, not greater depth of understanding. The best plan fits on one page, and any manager who cannot meet this standard should be given another job. In a multibusiness corporation, moreover, a CEO has no choice—a deep involvement in operating details is simply not feasible. This is not to say that executives should slight implementation. Exceptional performance demands equal attention to both strategy and implementation.

The corollary to standardized format in plan presentation is common language. On the hopeful premise that plans will be communicated to many members of the organization (as well as appropriate other members of the community of stakeholders), a standard lexicon greatly facilitates comprehension.[8]

Strategic planning is sometimes embraced so that managers can emulate their peers, assuring, as with quality, excellence, issue management, and other historic shibboleths, that they are *au courant*. More often, however, managers are attempting to respond to a need for greater discipline in decision-making. Indeed, over a period of time many corporations can move from the stage of managing by *impulse*, a stage characterized by reactive attitudes, introspection, irrationality, incoherent decision making, and muddling through, to the state of *managing by strategy*. When a firm manages by strategy, the organization is proactive, rather than the victim of its environment. The focus shifts from inside the firm (plant and equipment) to outside the firm (customers, competitors, suppliers). Rather than being driven by the personality of its managers, the firm responds to the demands of the total ecosystem.

The prelude to managing by strategy often requires a period in which rigorous analytical disciplines are imposed. But market research, matrix displays, resource allocation algorithms—all are in a sense subterfuges to get managers to think more rationally and strategically. Ultimately, like the tennis player who practices for many years until his stroke becomes grooved, these mechanisms and processes are internalized and the formalism of strategic planning can be abandoned. Formal strategic planning, in fact, can be viewed in most corporations as merely a transitory phenomenon imposed as the firm gropes its way forward.[9] Much of planning is still heuristic ("Let's try it and see what happens; after all, it seems like common sense"), as opposed to algorithmic ("If we do this, we know what will happen").[10]

Resistance to planning is pervasive. The opponents of a formalized approach may argue that the system cannot be understood, or that uncontrolled political or economic factors defy the aim of planning. Still others prefer to rely on intuition, disavowing the need to be rational or systematic. But planning is neither foolish and dangerous nor evil, and it is not necessary to live a reactive existence. Effective planning does facilitate good decisions, and evidence continues to accumulate that firms with formal planning systems exhibit superior long-term financial performance, both relative to the industry and in absolute terms.[11] But organizations contemplating a virgin effort in formal planning need to be cautious. Important considerations include simplicity, flexibility, top management support, and a tolerance for imperfections in the early editions of the plan.

MEASUREMENT AND CONTROL

Once an organization has allocated resources to strategies, the implementation process begins. The measurement and control component of the managerial system provides information on whether progress is being made in accordance with expectations. The salient questions will include *what* to measure and *how often* to measure it.

The question of what to measure has been dealt with previously; both financial and strategic parameters need to be tracked. Harold Geneen, the autocratic former chairman of ITT, makes a persuasive argument for focus on numerical data:

> numbers are your controls, and you read them until your mind reels or until you come across one number or set of numbers that stand out from all the rest, demanding your attention and getting it. What you are seeking is comprehension of the numbers: what they mean. . . The truth is that the drudgery of the numbers will make you free.[12]

Or, to cite Kenneth Olsen, chairman of DEC,

> pray about the P&L statement. If the P&L is not so simple you can remember every line . . . you don't know what you want and you don't know what your plans are.[13]

The necessary precursor to measuring financial performance is a sound budget. But programs based on strategy often require support from several units of the organization. New product development, for example, a vital strategy for many businesses, requires contributions from R&D, manufacturing, and marketing. As a result, functional activities and budgets must be linked to business strategies. This requires that managers establish a budget by *strategy*, in addition to the conventional process of budgeting that assigns resources by *function* (Figure 7–1).

Figure 7-1. Linking Strategy to Budget.

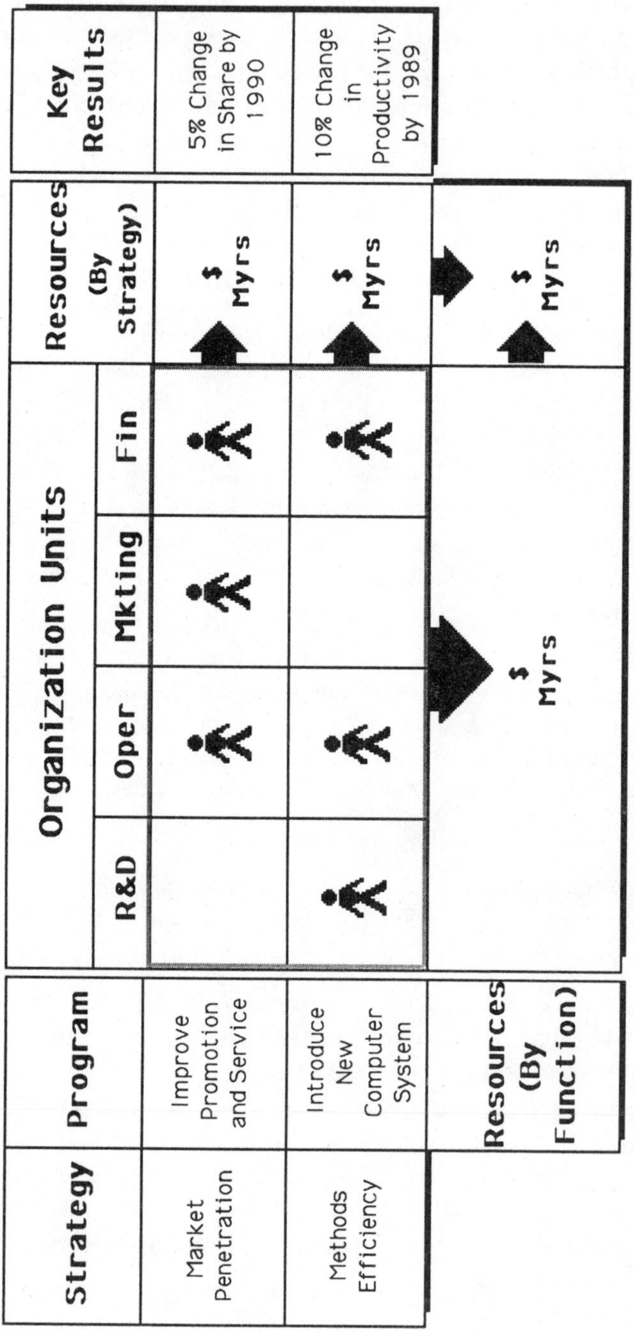

Strategy	Program	Organization Units				Resources (By Strategy)	Key Results
		R&D	Oper	Mkting	Fin		
Market Penetration	Improve Promotion and Service		«●	«●	«●	↑ $ Myrs	5% Change in Share by 1990
Methods Efficiency	Introduce New Computer System	«●	«●		«●	↑ $ Myrs	10% Change in Productivity by 1989
Resources (By Function)			→ $ Myrs			► $ Myrs	

Measuring financial performance is not enough; strategic measures of performance are the necessary complement to financial measures. Although satisfying the customer may be a continuing requirement, in every stage of an industry's evolution at least one other performance measure probably stands out as critical to the future of the firm— that is, to the successful implementation of its strategy. For example, in a startup high-technology business, managers are concerned primarily about whether the product will improve technical performance— providing reliability, speed, or efficiency, for example. In the growth stage when competitors vie for new customers, the key measure of performance is probably market share. When the name of the game shifts to price, managers worry primarily about production cost or capacity utilization. And in the end game, cash flow may be the only thing that matters. In all stages of the industry's development, whatever the measure, practical strategists understand that performance must always be measured *relative to competitors'.*

The frequency of measurement should obviously be a matter of how stable and predictable performance is. In a dynamic and volatile industry such as computer software, frequent monitoring of performance is appropriate. More stable situations (such as regulated industries) demand less frequent monitoring.

Many organizations have highly developed measurement systems, but they fail to go beyond the monitoring of performance to correct deviation from expectations. From a systems theory perspective, measurement provides the information necessary to complete the feedback loop (control) that either amplifies or attenuates the activities of the oganization. When variance from expected performance (budget, schedule, quality, for example) exceeds the permissible amount, the error (the response) signals the need for a change in other elements of the managerial system. Thus, a well-designed control system will specify how much variance is tolerable, who is responsible for diagnosis of the problem, and what corrective action is to be taken.

MANAGEMENT SELECTION AND DEVELOPMENT

The ability of any organization to implement strategy is vitally dependent on the quality of management. Thus, the managerial system must give extraordinary priority to selecting the right managers and helping them develop to meet future challenges.

Management Selection

Many corporations in the 1960s adopted the position that management was a skill that could be transferred easily from one situation to another. Thus, provided a manager had mastered the fundamentals of planning, organizing, integrating, and measuring (or whatever the particular corporation identified as the essential managerial skills), he or she could manage any kind of business. As a result, managers in large corporations were shifted with impunity from stable capital-intensive manufacturing businesses to volatile service businesses and back. The results in most cases were less than impressive.

Each business requires a manager who is adept at carrying out strategies appropriate for that business. For the new venture, for example, we seek an entrepreneur, a manager who feels comfortable with ambiguity and uncertainty, and who is willing to take large risks. But large, mature businesses play a different game. For such businesses, a "critical administrator" makes more sense—a manager who is concerned about (and enjoys) maximizing efficiency.

Business history suggests that the entrepreneurs who start businesses are rarely able to manage the business as it moves to the next stage. They continue to be interested in innovation and new product development when efficiency becomes important. They continue to function in an informal participative mode when the corporation needs structure and clear direction from a leader.

Steve Jobs's involuntary displacement by John Scully at Apple Computer illustrates the natural evolution of managerial types in a growing organization. Mitch Kapor's voluntary yielding to Jim Manzi at Lotus Development Corporation after it broke through the $300 million sales level is another example, in this instance triggered by Kapor's recognition that, although he might still be competent to manage the corporation, his interests remained in entrepreneurship. Few successful entrepreneurs exhibit this degree of insight.

Managerial inflexibility is demonstrated as well by managers who attempt to move in the other direction. Thus, managers of large, mature businesses who have succeeded by imposing strong control systems will have little patience with the unpredictable outbursts of entrepreneurs. The classic example of this scenario occurs often in large, mature corporations seeking to revitalize themselves by diversifying into high-technology entrepreneurial ventures. Who should manage the first of these brave new enterprises? A familiar response is to pick the corporation's "best and most experienced" manager, an individual accustomed to implementing with vigor all the strategies necessary to win in a mature industry—all the strategies that assure failure in the new venture. This may also explain why, despite the attempts of large firms to foster "intrapreneurialism," innovation occurs primarily outside the corporation in small, new ventures.

Management Development

The guideline for hiring or assigning managers is to make sure the person possesses the skills needed to perform effectively. Management development allows a manager to develop new skills or enhance existing skills that will enable him or her to take on new or different responsibilities and roles within the organization.

In small enterprises, managers invariably assume the responsibility for their own development. Formal management development programs make their appearance later, when they are viewed both as educational activities and as socializing devices, rituals that help inculcate a particular set of corporte values and norms. Corporations like IBM and GE have established corporate policies that require managers to partake of at least forty hours of formal training annually.

It is not realistic to expect that management development (formal or informal) can prepare managers for different types of businesses, unless they have strategic similarities. Entrepreneurs are not equipped psychologically to run declining businesses. Nor do managers of large, mature commodity businesses feel comfortable running new ventures. But both can learn to appreciate the important variables in other kinds of businesses, and thus prepare for positions of greater responsibility within the firm. (It is easier for managers to move up the corporation than to move across the corporation.) In addition, managers can always learn skills that will help them implement strategy more effectively.

REWARD SYSTEMS

Since implementation is always improved when members of the organization are rewarded for results, the management literature is replete with theories of motivation. In Frederick Taylor's model of scientific management, motivation and reward were incidental variables in the

Figure 7–2. The Motivation Model.

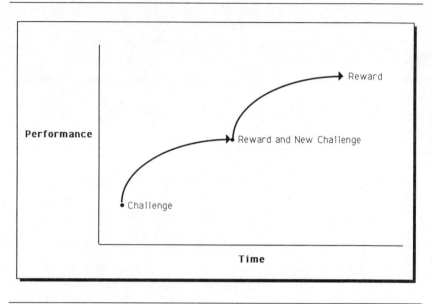

management process; the effective manager allocated human resources in the same way that physical or fiscal resources were allocated to maximize the efficiency of the firm. With the advent of the human potential movement, social psychologists such as Douglas McGregor (Theory X and Theory Y) and Frederick Herzberg took cognizance of the strong correlation between productivity and motivation.

Among contemporary organizational behaviorists, expectancy theory has strong support. This model hypothesizes that individuals perceive a certain relationship between their efforts and the resultant performance. They believe, furthermore, that their performance will yield a certain outcome (reward). The perceived relationships between effort, performance, and outcome represent the individual's *expectancy*. Their *valence* refers to the value placed by the individual on higher performance and rewards.

Most of the current explanations of motivation can be summarized in a simple model (Figure 7–2) that relates challenge, performance, and reward to one another in an ascending spiral. This model of management only works if the challenge is clearly articulated, the expected performance is understood (explicit measures are set forth and agreed upon), and the reward is proportional to performance. The reward system in any organization must support and reinforce the behavior necessary to carry out strategy. The challenge, in other words, must specify explicitly the appropriate kind of expected behavior.

Managers attempting to apply this (or any) model must also recognize again the principle of differentiation; that is, different businesses experience different challenges, they need to implement different strategies, and they have different expected outcomes. A corporate reward system therefore must recognize the singularity of individual organizational units.

SUMMARY

Implementation necessitates that managers ground abstract strategy statements in the reality of action programs. This entails specific assignment of responsibility and accountability for performance. But even the most carefully plotted program will founder if the organization lacks the right managerial system—the appropriate organization, information systems, measurement systems, rewards, and the right culture and managerial climate.

The overarching theme for the design of managerial systems is differentiation. A common corporate fallacy is to install a standardized set of systems to govern the behavior of all the activities of the organization. But since there are no universal systems, the practical strategist will select and put in place individualized systems that fit the particular strategic need of the business and corporation. The managerial systems specification changes in all dimensions as strategy is modified to accommodate the changing environment. As Herman Melville has noted, there are indeed some enterprises in which a careful disorderliness is the true method. But it is equally true that other organizations and their strategy demand critical administration in order to be successful.

Systems that do not fit the strategic requirements of the enterprise interfere with strategy implementation. They increase the amount of managerial energy that is expended in conforming to unnatural constraints, and the risk increases that the strategy will take longer to carry out, cost more, or fail. Congruent systems, by contrast, facilitate strategy implementation. Even in a mature business, for example, entrepreneurial behavior can be encouraged by providing freedom for constructive action, incentive sytems that encourage response to opportunities, and value systems that demand performance but tolerate justifiable failure.[14]

Table 7–1 recapitulates the changes to be expected in the important managerial systems as strategy evolves.

Table 7–1.   Managerial Systems Analysis.

Strategic Emphasis	Primary Objectives	Organization	Communication and Information Systems
New Venture/ start-up	Start up and survive	Organization is small but growing rapidly in response to new needs; marketing function often grows rapidly because of push for market share. Rapid growth, however, produces organizational instability; structure is informal and changes frequently, responsibilities may not be clearly defined.	Emphasis is on rapid response, information system is informal and designed for specific business. Reporting is largely qualitative, un-systematic, and market oriented. Few formal policies and procedures exist.
Market penetration	Improve competitive positions, growth, market share.	Organization is less open to change; structure is a function of competitive forces and strategies. Informal relationships emerge within the formal structure. Increased variety of tasks produce greater complexity and hierarchy. Organization becomes formal; task differentiation is stressed.	Formal communications stress planning; informal communications empha-size response to short-term opportunities. Formal and informal systems come into balance but formal systems become more detailed and quantitative as business size and complexity increase.
Efficiency/ segmentation	Maintain competitive position, profit, cash flow, efficiency.	Task integration is a key goal. Established report-ing relationships, career paths, customer and sup-plier relationships make the organization resis-tant to change. Business may be multifunctional, multidivisional, and multilevel resulting in very complex structures.	Coordination and con-trol are more important as organization becomes complex and strategies become internally focused. Communica-tions stress coordination and control, become more systematic and quantitative; become more one-way than two-way.
Consolidation/ rationalization	Cash flow, survival, harvest.	Organization is large but starts to diminish in size. Control functions are of great importance. Although structure is formal, rationalization begins to reduce com-plexity. As a result, organization may be less stable.	Communications emphasize quantitative control; balance sheet information is presented in a very structured manner. Many policies and procedures are promulgated.

Table 7–1. Managerial Systems Analysis. (Cont.)

Planning Systems	Measurement and Control Systems	Reward System	Management Development
Emphasis on new products and customers. Planning horizon tends to be long, although planning cycles may be short because of rapidly changing conditions. Plans often cover wide range of options.	System focuses on markets and product development, identifying areas for rapid response. Measurements may be frequent but tend not to be precise; a limited number of measurement parameters are utilized.	Incentive compensation is high relative to fixed compensation; high risk often demands larger incentive and larger rewards. Performance measures stress growth rather than profit. Compensation system tends to be informal and flexible.	Formal management development programs and succession paths do not exist. Little specialized training is available. Management skills and resources are drawn from both within and outside the firm.
Planning is concerned with products and programs to compete in the marketplace. Planning horizon coincides with investment payback period. Approach to planning becomes more structured but remains flexible.	Focus is on marketing and manufacturing. Measurements are taken less frequently, but isolation of key data is an important control function. Multiple performance measures require coordination between controllers and line management.	Deferred compensation diminishes in favor of current rewards. Promotion and compensation both are factors in compensation. Benefits depend on individual and group performance.	Rapid growth rates require infusion of management to those businesses having viable competitive positions. Formal development programs begin. Growth in this period may be constrained due to lack of management or inability to acquire outside resources.
Plans begin to focus on internal efficiency and are prepared by product line, market and business function. Planning horizon typically 3–5 years as industry becomes more predictable and opportunities for radical strategies diminish. Planning system is very formal.	The system stresses manufacturing and financial performance. Regular periods of measurement are more widely spaced. Control and information systems are highly developed, making it easier to run the business by numbers.	Rewards are tailored to position, and include factors such as position level, span of control, and performance. Rewards reflect specific strategy or managerial mission. Promotion paths and compensation are well defined. Internal competition is fostered.	Management supply is self-sufficient. Formal development, education and promotional programs are in place. Little outside hiring except for specialized needs. Professional staff development more important than managerial development.
Planning emphasizes plant performance. Very short planning horizon, often influenced by lead time on new investment. Planning process formal; calendar is fixed.	Emphasis is on financial performance that maximizes profits and cash flow. Measures are few but fixed. The level of detail diminishes as product lines and markets are rationalized. Reporting period may increase.	Incentive compensation is less important than fixed compensation; incentive compensation based largely on control and financial performance. Compensation system is formal and rigid.	Oversupply of qualified staff. Turnover increases as personal ambitions are thwarted, unless opportunity is made available elsewhere in the parent organization. Management development deemphasized.

NOTES

1. Reported in *PIMSletter 34*, Strategic Planning Institute, Cambridge, MA, 1985.
2. Alfred D. Chandler, Jr. has described at length the evolution of the multi-divisional organization in *Strategy and Structure* (Cambridge, MA: The M.I.T. Press, 1984).
3. See Richard E. Caves, "Industrial Organization, Corporate Strategy and Structure," *Journal of Economic Literature, 18* (March 1980).
4. We may be doomed, otherwise, to wander forever seeking the correct information in Borges' library of infinite shelves.
5. G.T. Allison, *Essence of Decision: Explaining the Cuban Missile Crisis* (Boston: Little-Brown, 1971).
6. Japanese firms, however, have long been advocates of *nemawashi*, a process of building consensus before decisions are made.
7. Elliott Jaques suggests that long time horizons reflect the superior cognitive power of executives (Walter Kiechel III, "How Executives Think," *Fortune*, February 4, 1985, p. 127); Matsushita is said to have prepared a 250-year plan for his corporation.
8. Benjamin Whorf, the noted U.S. linguist, has postulated that language affects perception, and therefore speakers of different language experience the world differently. Thus, we are prisoners of the structure of our language—how we think will be influenced by the language in which we think.
9. In the psychiatric lexicon, the strategic plan itself can be viewed as a transitional object to be discarded after the individual achieves enough sense of security to cope with the outside world.
10. Henry Mintzberg identifies an entrepreneurial mode, an adaptive mode, and a planning mode for organizations in various stages of development. See "Strategy-making in Three Modes," *California Management Review* (Winter 1973).
11. L.C. Rhyne, "Strategic Planning and Financial Performance," *Strategic Management Journal*, 7, no. 5 (September–October 1986).
12. "The Case for Managing by Numbers," *Fortune*, October 1, 1984.
13. Kenneth H. Olsen, "The Education of an Entrepreneur," *The New York Times*, July 19, 1987, p. 2.
14. R. Jeffery Ellis, *Managing Strategy in the Real World*, (Lexington, MA: Lexington Books, 1988), p. 292.

8 MEASURING PERFORMANCE

BUSINESS PERFORMANCE

Progress in implementing business strategy must be monitored on the basis of several financial and strategic measures, although the specific parameters vary by business. In addition, future performance expectations must be complemented by a realistic assessment of risk.

Financial Measures

Two measures of historic and projected financial performance should dominate the measurement system: profitability and cash flow. The simplest useful measure of profitability for a business is *return on net assets* (RONA).[1] Return should ideally be expressed after tax, and assets should be net of intangibles such as depreciation and goodwill.

$$\text{Return on net assets} = \text{Income after tax/Net assets,}$$

or

$$\text{RONA} = \text{IAT/NA,}$$

where   IAT = Income after tax, and
         NA = Fixed assets + Working capital.

157

At the corporate level, this expression is equivalent to return on investment (ROI), where investment is defined as the sum of stockholders' equity and long-term debt. The income after tax calculation normally imputes the corporate tax rate to the business. If the businesses are heterogeneous, however, estimates of real tax rates may need to be used, especially if some units benefit from depletion allowances or tax shelters, or if liquidity is constrained by repatriation laws. Interest expense is usually not included, as it can be assumed to be a corporate financing cost.

Several alternative measures of business profitability are used by corporations, including the essentially identical *return on assets* (ROA), *return on invested capital*, or *return on capital employed* (ROCE), expressed as follows:

Return on capital employed = Income after tax/Capital employed,

or

$$ROCE = IAT/CE,$$

where   IAT = Income after tax, and
CE = Capital employed (Fixed assets + Current assets).

Both ROCE and ROA measure the productive use of all of the firm's assets.

The return earned by the business, no matter how computed, must be sufficient to repay the corporation for the use of its capital. As a result, *residual income* is calculated in some corporations to take explicit account of the cost of capital used by the business. In this calculation, residual income (RI) is defined as follows:

$$RI = IAT - k*NA,$$

where k = Corporate cost of capital, and
NA = Net assets assigned to the business.

The after-tax corporate cost of capital is the weighted average of its after-tax debt cost and equity capital cost:

$$k = pk_d + (1-p)k_e,$$

where p is the proportion of total assets represented by debt, and $(1-p)$ is the proportion of equity.

The implicit premise in this measure is that the business unit must earn a return sufficient to repay the corporation for the use of its capital. Satisfactory performance is achieved, therefore, when residual income is greater than zero.

An equivalent philosophy entails the use of *return on notional equity*. In this approach, each business unit is assumed to have the capital structure of the parent corporation, and hence the same obligation to earn a return in excess of the corporation's cost of capital.

Most corporations using these approaches assume the cost of capital to be identical for each of the businesses in its portfolio, a simplifying assumption, since k will be higher for risky businesses than for mature, stable businesses. Attempting to devise a precise cost of capital for each business often precipitates bitter managerial disputes. Nevertheless, the distortions in resource allocation that can arise from ignoring this matter can be important. (See Chapter 6 for further discussion.)

Calculations of business unit profitability, however expressed, are inevitably colored by the underlying accounting assumptions. Without violating any generally accepted accounting principles, a manager can produce violent swings in reported earnings by varying policy on R&D (expensed or capitalized), inventory (FIFO or LIFO), depreciation (straight line or accelerated), bad debt reserve (conservative or aggressive), and accelerated sales or delayed purchases, to cite just a few options. Replacement accounting methods introduce still another possibility for changing reported profitability.

For all these reasons, *cash flow* (or *funds flow*) is often a more useful measure than profitability, avoiding as it does all the ambiguity resulting from accounting assumptions. Managers of small businesses have no difficulty appreciating this point; in large corporations, unfortunately, managers almost never see cash. Nevertheless, whatever the size of the business, in the long run managers must return cash to the investor, not net income.

Since the term *cash flow* is loosely applied, great care is required when making comparisons or interpreting financial data. I recommend that managers distinguish between *operating cash flow* and *total cash flow*, using the following definitions:

Operating cash flow = Net profit + Noncash charges.

This calculation shows us approximately how much cash is being produced by operating the business. The largest noncash charge, of course, is usually depreciation. A precise calculation of operating cash flow would simply subtract cost from revenue, assuming the firm operated on a cash basis. Because most firms have adopted accrual accounting systems, however, such a simple calculation is not possible.

Operating cash flow does not represent the total source and use of funds at the level of the business. Monies flow to acquire or dispose of plant and equipment, increase or decrease inventory, accounts receivable, and accounts payable. When these additional sources and uses are considered, the total cash flow becomes the sum of operating cash flow corrected for cash expended (or received) when assets are increased (or reduced). In other words,

$$\text{Total cash flow } = \text{ Operating cash flow } + \Delta \text{ assets.}$$

This total cash flow represents the free cash available for use by the corporation for reinvestment, dividend payment, or changes in the firm's capital structure.[2]

The theoretically correct measure of financial performance for a business, of course, is the present value of future cash flows, that is, the present value on a discounted cash flow basis. In principle, therefore, we should also be able to evaluate the present value (and thus the economic merit) of every proposed business strategy. Cash flow is the ultimate link between business strategy and financial performance.

The *reinvestment ratio*, R, describes the degree to which the business uses corporate cash or contributes cash to the corporation. The corporate analog to reinvestment ratio is $(1 - \text{dividend payout})$. For the business, we define reinvestment as follows:

$$R = \text{ Change in assets/Operating cash flow.}$$

A business having $R = 1$ will reinvest each dollar generated from business operations. When R is greater than 1, the business will reinvest more cash than it generates; this is typical for embryonic and growth businesses or for any business adopting growth strategies. An R less than 1 is experienced when operating cash flow exceeds the investment needs of the business. Values of R less than 0 occur when the business is reducing its asset base. Plotting the historic and expected future values of R and RONA will show the relationship between resource utilization and expected profitability.

Managers usually find it prudent to assess the financial performance of a business strategy using additional measures of performance, such as historic comparisons, ratio analysis, and peer comparisons.

Historic versus Projected Results.   Although projections beyond three years often become an exercise in trend extrapolation, business unit performance obviously cannot be assessed on the basis of one year's results. A comparison of projections with recent history will identify any inflections in performance that need to be clarified. The use of indexes for each of the major financial statement items facilitates these comparisons.

Ratio Analysis.   Performance in absolute dollars will be the ultimate criterion for acceptable results. But ratios give important clues as to viability of the strategy that has been (or will be) undertaken. Each of the important profit and loss or balance sheet items can be treated in this way. Similarly, certain business strategies need to produce predictable trends in key ratios. Embarking on a vigorous program to improve market share, for example, typically requires significant increases in R&D, marketing, inventory, and receivables per dollar of sales. The corollary to this recommendation is that businesses must select ratios to track that will reflect the proposed strategy.

Peer Comparisons.   Rarely should a business unit attempt to emulate the financial performance of its competitors, since they will often be entertaining different strategies and operating from different competitive positions. But these comparisons can give strong clues about competitors' value chains and strategies, and may suggest that the limits of efficiency or effectiveness are beyond those previously set. A contemporary approach to peer comparison is designated as benchmarking. In the benchmarking technique, the costs associated with each of the elements of the value chain are compared within the industry.

We can now ask an important question: Is financial performance congruent with strategy? As suggested earlier, the expected financial performance of a business will be heavily influenced by the maturity of its industry, its competitive position, and its strategy. As a result, different businesses exhibit different financial characteristics. Nevertheless, norms for both profitability and cash flow can be identified as illustrated in Figure 8–1.

Under normal circumstances, both RONA or ROCE and cash flow peak in maturity, although the specific situation alters the strength of this correlation. For example, cash flow may be different from normally

Figure 8–1. Strategic and Financial Congruence.

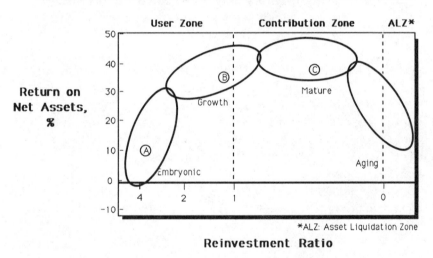

*ALZ: Asset Liquidation Zone

anticipated in a mature industry if the business has low capital needs, or if high margins continue to be realized, or if price competition or regulatory intervention depresses margins.

The relationship between RONA and *R* is most useful for testing the congruence between strategy and financial performance. Consider the example of Figure 8–1. Business A has a tenable position in an early growth industry. The RONA of 10 percent and reinvestment ratio of 4.0

Figure 8–2. Business Unit's Financial Profile.

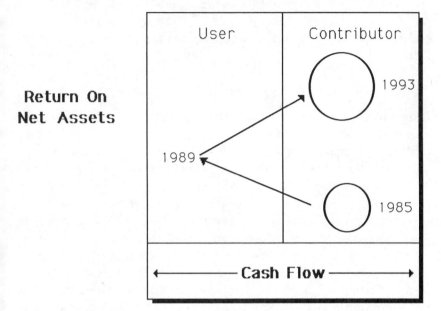

are inconsistent with strategic condition. The tenable position and low RONA suggest that this business is spending aggressively in hope of improving its competitive position before the industry matures. (Another hypothesis, of course, is that the business is simply out of control.)

Business B has a strong position in a late growth industry. It shows reasonable return and is close to breakeven on cash flow. Both RONA and *R* are consistent with its strategic position.

Business C holds a favorable position in a growth industry. The high RONA and positive cash flow suggest that investment may not be sufficient to maintain competitive position.

Stronger businesses will generate greater operating cash flow because of their higher profitability. Aggressive strategies implemented to improve long-term competitive position tend to reduce cash flow and impair short-term profitability in some cases, as illustrated in Figure 8–2. If the strategy is successful, these short term effects are offset by long-term gains in both cash flow and return on capital.

The case of Miller Brewing (Chapter 5 Appendix) provides a classic illustration of this situation; improving industry position from number 7 to 2 in the 1970s required an infusion of enormous amounts of cash. Profit margins declined dramatically during this period and cash flow was negative. Not until the early 1980s, when the growth strategy was moderated, did profit margins and cash flow return to more normal levels. Nevertheless, on a discounted cash flow basis, the cost of the strategy appears to have substantially exceeded the value it produced for Miller.

Measuring Strategic Performance

In many instances the demands placed on many managers for short-term financial performance have led to sacrifices of strategic performance on the altar of profit margin or return on investment. But the manager who cuts his R&D budget, defers critical advertising and promotion for a new product, or postpones strategically essential capital expenditures, will in the long run lose competitive position. This kind of managerial behavior will produce at the corporate level what investment analysts refer to as low quality earnings.

As a result, managers must also be held accountable for achieving strategic objectives. This really means simply "Don't cut the budget if the strategy suffers." To this end, some executives have adopted the meritorious practice of correcting the net income figures reported by their business managers for any significant underspending on strategic programs. Such intervention is necessary to correct for the short-term tenure of many general managers (often no more than two or three years) and to improve the "quality" of earnings.

For the overall business, the most important strategic measure of importance is competitive position. That is, the ultimate measure of performance in the long run is whether we have strengthened our position relative to competitors—increased our competitive advantage. For the individual strategies of the business, a number of appropriate measures can be adopted, including market share, product or service quality, and new product introduction. Thus, for example, if a business strategy is to improve performance by new product innovation, counting the number of new products is a straightforward approach to performance measurement and may take precedence over RONA or other financial measures.

CORPORATE PERFORMANCE

The ultimate accolade for a corporation is to be designated as "excellent" or "high-performing" or "leading." But these terms are ambiguous. We must first establish appropriate criteria for excellence and then agree on the standards (operational definitions) against which excellence can be measured. Common criteria for performance evaluation are the following:

Performance Relative to Historic Performance.   Can we match or exceed the performance recorded in an earlier era of the organization? This may prove to be a snare and delusion, as historic performance may no longer be achievable in the current environment. For that matter, performance in 1986 may be far below what is possible in 1990. In either event the performance of the firm may need to be measured using different factors in different time periods.

Performance Relative to Industry Peers.   This criterion is popular with many managers. Unfortunately, a firm may have no peers within its industry. Comparisons of IBM versus DEC or GM versus Ford and Chrysler do not have great validity; the other competitors within the industry have different resources, are following different strategies, and have achieved greater or lesser competitive standing in the marketplace. Furthermore, the industry as a whole may be realizing unacceptable returns.

Performance Relative to Objectives and Goals.   Is the plan being implemented efficiently? Managers find this to be a more useful criterion, provided, of course, that the objectives are appropriate. This is a critical caveat, since too often goals and objectives either understate potential performance or represent unattainably difficult standards.

Performance Relative to Potential.   Is the ultimate potential of the organization being realized? This is the best standard, despite the inherent difficulties in setting performance targets. It establishes absolute goals, rather than the relative goals set in other measures. And it challenges the organization and its members to strive for performance that may never have been achieved or considered before. It is my firm belief that most organizations and individuals operate at no more than 30 percent of their potential.

As in the case of business unit performance, total corporate performance has strategic and financial dimensions. In the 1950s GE attempted to look at itself in terms of eight "key result areas" that were designed to measure both dimensions:

- Financial: Profitability
               Productivity

- Strategic: Market position
               Product leadership
               Personnel development
               Employee attitudes
               Public responsibility
               Balance between short-range and long-range goals

This book encourages a multidimensional approach to measuring corporate performance that includes financial and strategic dimensions plus one other: risk and vulnerability. Each is described in the balance of this chapter.

Financial Measures

Managers of public corporations must allocate resources in a way that produces satisfactory financial performance. Growth, profitability, capital structure, and dividend policy are not independent variables, as the growth equation illustrates. Thus, assuming a constant relationship between sales/investment and profit/sales, the allowable growth will be determined by the cash available from internal operations and external sources. In the simplest example, when there is no debt and no payment of dividends, return on net assets must equal sales growth if cash flow is to be adequate. Gordon Donaldson[3] applies these relationships to develop an acceptable combination of growth and profitability under a variety of assumptions. Consider the case, for example, of a corporate financial strategy that includes a debt-to-equity ratio of 0.50 and a dividend payout of 0.30, assuming an after tax interest cost of 6 percent. A sales growth rate of 16 percent in this situation will create cash deficits unless the after tax return on net assets exceeds 15 percent.

The appropriate elements of financial performance at the corporate level are return on equity, return on investment, earnings growth, cash flow, and shareholders' value. Earnings per share is a flawed, albeit popular, performance criterion; it ignores the assets required to generate earnings and is biased by various accounting assumptions, including the failure to capitalize long-term investments in R&D or marketing.

Return on Equity. From a stockholder's point of view, return on equity (ROE) represents the single most important measure of corporate performance. Since ROE reflects how effectively the corporation utilizes shareholders' investment, the market value of the firm (stock price) is most sensitive to changes in this variable.

Return on equity (ROE) is defined as follows:

Return on equity = Income after tax/Stockholders' equity,

or

$$ROE = IAT/E,$$

where   IAT = income after tax,
          E = stockholders' equity (book value).

At a minimum, any corporation must earn a return equal to the cost of its invested capital. The cost of equity capital, k_e, defined according to the capital asset pricing model (CAPM), is as follows:

Cost of equity capital = Risk-free return + Risk premium,

or

$$k_e = R_f + \beta (R_m - R_f),$$

where R_f = risk-free return
                       R_m = market return
             $(R_m - R_f)$ = risk premium
                       β = risk multiplier for a particular stock.

The risk-free return is the real rate of interest plus the inflation rate. Using long-term Treasury bills as the standard, R_f in mid-1988 was 9.03 percent, while R_m, the average return on corporate equity, was 16.14 percent.

The risk multiplier for an individual business reflects the systematic risk for the business or corporation relative to the stock market as a whole. The market as a whole is assigned a β of one. A business having a β less than one will exhibit less variability than the market as a whole. Businesses having high variability in cash flow will be assigned β values greater than one. Industries also exhibit different degrees of risk, and hence can be assigned β values that imply the need to earn a higher or lower return on equity. Industry values of β currently range between about 0.50 for regulated industries (electric utilities, for example) and 1.8 for volatile high-technology industries (computer peripherals, for example).

The cost of equity capital can also be estimated as follows:

Cost of equity capital = Dividend payout/Stock price + Earnings growth,

or

$$k_e = D/P + G,$$

where D = dividend payout
         P = stock price
         G = earnings growth.

Return on Investment.   The ability of the firm to utilize all the assets under its control is best described by its return on investment (ROI):

Return on investment = Income after tax/Investment.

Because we choose to define the firm's investment as the sum of its long-term debt and equity (rather than total assets), this formula can be stated more simply as

$$ROI = IAT/(D + E).$$

In this equation investment is equivalent to the total assets of the firm less current liabilities. Other measures of performance, such as net margin (return on sales), are imperfect surrogates for return on investment, because they ignore the critical role of assets, in the form of property, plant, and equipment or working capital, in generating revenue and profit.

Earnings Growth.   This measure of performance correlates strongly with return on equity, although high return on equity will not produce high growth unless the investment base of the firm is increasing. Improvements in earnings growth (see the corporate financing discussion in Chapter 6) can thus be achieved in two very different ways:

1. By increasing financial leverage (if the marginal return is greater than the cost of the debt)
2. By maximizing the reinvestment of free cash—in other words, by reducing dividend payout to the shareholder.

Certainly these two approaches can also be used concurrently.

Cash Flow.   The investment needs of the firm must be satisfied by the combination of cash generated internally, i.e., from the businesses of the firm, and cash generated externally, that is, from new debt or equity. But the amount of funds that can be sought externally is ultimately limited by cost. As debt increases (as a percent of total capital), the lender's financial risk increases and the cost to the borrower goes up. Similarly, the cost of new equity may be excessive if investors do not view the firm experiencing positive cash flow from earnings. Suffice it to say, then, that corporations must generate cash flow, be it positive or negative, that is consistent with the strategic position of the portfolio of the corporation.

Stockholders' Value.   The clearest indicator of the value assigned by the investor to the corporation (its economic value) is the market price of the stock relative to the book value.[4] This relationship not only makes sense theoretically but also has had the benefit of extensive empirical validation. When a firm's return on equity equals its cost of capital (ROE = k_e), the market value of the firm will be equal to its book value. In the simplest case, therefore, we may impute low stock price to unsatisfactory return on equity. In fact, when the return on equity of the firm falls to zero, the market value of the firm will fall to its liquidation value.

If a firm's earnings exceed its cost of capital, additional value will be ascribed to the firm, and the value of its stock will rise, particularly if financial performance can be sustained over a significant time period (volatility of earnings will result in lower multiples). The average price/book ratio of the S&P 400 in mid 1988 was 2.10, corresponding to an ROE of 16.14 percent.

If the anticipated growth in earnings is high, a further premium will be assigned to the firm's value. This explains why computer firms may sell at higher price-to-book ratios than textile companies, even when returns on equity are similar. The relationship among these variables is shown in Figure 8–3. Earlier empirical models of valuation used by investment banks attempt to correlate *P/E* ratios, EPS growth, and dividend policy (Figure 8–4).

Firms positioned in industries having low slope (weak dependence of market price on return on equity) may aspire to diversify into high-slope industries (that is, industries in which market value is more sensitive to return on equity). This is a reasonable strategy if the entry

Figure 8–3. Relative Stock Valuation.

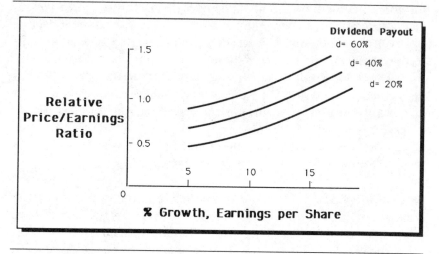

Figure 8–4. Correlating Shareholders' Value with Profitability.

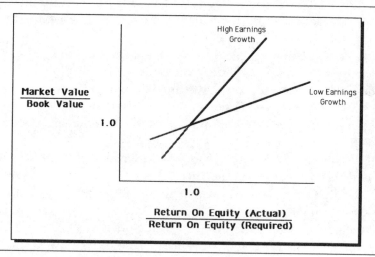

barriers are surmountable (that is, if the ante is not too large), and if management can tolerate the higher risks associated with high growth and diversity.

Although the price-to-book value ratio of a firm has a high correlation with the firm's return on equity relative to its cost of capital, the calculation of ROE is based on accrual accounting. As a result the calculation ignores the possibility that a high ROE may be achieved by a harvesting strategy that reduces the investment prematurely. The ROE calculation also overestimates the profitability of a business that uses highly depreciated assets.

Bernard Riemann and others prefer a present value calculation of profitability.[5] In this method, present value is determined by discounting the projected cash flows for the proposed strategy of the business and its expected residual value at the end of the planning period. Although theoretically sound, a present value calculation requires forecasts of both future cash flow (no easier to forecast than future earnings) and discount rates (an even less predictable parameter).

The present value of the business can also be described by the Q ratio, where Q is the present value of assets (the equivalent of market value) divided by the replacement value of the assets. A Q ratio > 1 means that the market values assets at more than their cost—and the corporation is thus given a signal to increase its investment. When $Q < 1$, the incentive to invest is reduced. The use of replacement value rather than book value also corrects for the bias inherent in comparing one business to another that may have acquired assets at different times.

A number of analysts have established a high correlation between Q and spread (defined as the difference between return on equity and cost of equity capital), even greater than the correlation between market-to-book ratio and spread.[6] As a consequence, Q can be used to determine the potential contribution of strategy to stock price. A related methodology calculates the value return on investment (VROI), where VROI measures the incremental change in shareholders' value for each incremental investment dollar.

Some additional variables also affect shareholders' value:

1. *Volatile or unstable industries.* The performance of an individual firm may be clouded by the unstable or volatile nature of its industry. Recent examples of this phenomenon may be found in the sugar, airlines, and oil industries.

2. *Undervalued assets.* Stock price may be depressed by the firm's failure to utilize assets that have a high intrinsic value, such as oil or real estate.

3. *Stereotyping.* Firms labeled by the market as lackluster often conceal within their portfolios a number of exciting small businesses whose value is obscured by the characteristics of the rest of the portfolio.

A number of strategies suggest themselves to the public corporation experiencing these maladies. For the corporation earning less than its cost of capital, the solution is obvious: Improve performance, either by improving returns or by reducing the assets committed to low-return businesses. Firms in volatile or unstable industries may wish to consider diversification or going private. Firms with jewels buried in their portfolios need to consider the merit of spinning them off as independent public subsidiaries. Whatever the solution, firms with undervalued assets must either utilize them effectively or disinvest. Those that fail will inevitably fall prey to corporate raiders like Boone Pickens and Asher Edelman.

Strategic Measures

Sustained economic or financial performance entails that we give equal attention to strategic performance. The recommended measures of strategic performance include portfolio quality, productivity, innovation, and stakeholder relations.

Portfolio Quality.   A corporation's portfolio is usually dominated by assets managed by the businesses of the corportion. As a consequence, the quality of the portfolio as a whole depends on several dimensions:

Maturity.   Seeking an optimal mix of growth and mature businesses ensures that economic renewal can take place as the corporation replaces aging businesses by maturing growth businesses while maintaining adequate current cash flow. In financial terms such a portfolio provides a balance between negative and positive cash flow.

Competitive position.   The ideal portfolio contains businesses that occupy only strong or leading positions within their industries. This, of course, is the criterion expressed by Jack Welch in his demand that GE businesses be or quickly become either number 1 or number 2 in their industries. Most firms cannot hope to achieve this standard in the short term, but all can work on improving their portfolios gradually.

Risk.   The riskiness of a portfolio is sometimes expressed in terms of the quality of earnings it produces—that is, the degree to which it may be vulnerable to economic cycles or unforeseen discontinuities.

From the investors' point of view, a stable, increasing stream of earnings is most desirable. However, this view of the world tends to inhibit publicly held corporations from investing in research and development programs, in high risk ventures, and in other activities that offer significant long-term potential. The desire to satisfy investors must be balanced by the long-term needs of the markets in which the firm competes.

Productivity.   The survival of a corporation in the long run depends on maintaining productivity levels at least as high as the productivity of its family of competitors. In classic economic terms, this simply means maximizing output per unit of input. A surrogate for productivity can be supplied by the notion of value-added per employee. Other measures of productivity include sales per employee and unit output per employee. Superior corporations distinguish themselves by their high levels of managerial productivity, although admittedly this is not so easy to measure.

Innovation.   The excellent corporation finds new markets, develops new products and services, uncovers creative ways to motivate its employees. High levels of expenditure in R&D and marketing often reflect a commitment to innovation. Innovative corporations find new and better ways to perform at every level, and the great success of quality circles is simply another manifestation of this truth. And innovative corporations also adapt to changing circumstances with alacrity and grace.

Stakeholder Relations.   The managers of the corporation serve many masters. Although the shareholders constitute the legal owners of the firm, many other constituencies may lay claim to managerial attention. These include suppliers, customers, regulatory agencies, the board of directors, and various community groups. Slighting the needs of any one of these groups often has unfavorable consequences, including an unfavorable reputation.

To summarize, total performance is a multidimensional phenomenon, entailing financial and strategic components. These components reinforce one another to produce excellence (Figure 8–5).

ASSESSING RISK AND VULNERABILITY

A prudent manager assesses the risk associated with any proposed business or corporate strategy. This means determining whether the proposed outcomes are realistic, that is, have an acceptable probability of success.

Figure 8–5. Measures of Corporate Performance.

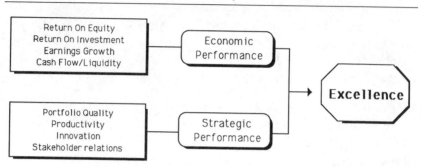

In the most highly developed form of such assessment (known as Monte Carlo analysis), the manager develops a probability distribution for each variable that has a significant bearing on outcome (revenues, costs, market share, and so on). The individual probability distributions are then compounded to produce an estimate of the probability of certain outcomes. The Monte Carlo method is little used today because of the dearth of data for all but a few industries.

A more common approach is sensitivity analysis. This method requires the manager to estimate the most probable results (50 percent probability, the expected value) and those that can be anticipated with 90 percent and 10 percent probability. Another version of sensitivity analysis is Strategic Scenario Analysis (SCENSIM). In this technique, multiple quantitative scenarios are translated into graphic "uncertainty clouds" to provide managers with a visual portrayal of the boundaries of possible performance.

From a qualitative point of view, important sources of risk include assumptions about the future, the intrinsic characteristics of the industry, the competitive position of the business, the strategy adopted by the firm, the managerial systems of the organization, and the realism of management expectations:

Future Assumptions.   Has management made reasonable assumptions regarding future conditions in the macroenvironment and microenvironment or are they overly optimistic or pessimistic?

Industry and Market.   Is the industry intrinsically risky and unpredictable (children's toys, cosmetics, high-fashion clothing, oil exploration, race horse breeding) or does it demonstrate good year-to-year stability (food service, basic commodities, specialty chemicals)? An embryonic industry, subject to the uncertainties of new competitors, new technologies, and other unknowns is riskier than a mature industry in which competitors and their strategies are better known and more predictable.

Competitive Position.   Does the position of the business allow it to exercise significant control over the industry and competitors? Or does its weak position make it especially vulnerable to fluctuations in demand or to the actions of competitors? Any strategy implemented from a weak position will entail higher risk than a similar strategy pursued from a stronger position.

Strategy.   Is the strategy set natural, given the competitive conditions of the industry? Or does it involve a direct assault upon competitors who will be asked to cede market share? Some strategies, such as new product development, are inherently riskier than others, such as improving efficiency or continuing to sell the same products to the same customers.

Managerial Systems.   Are the managerial systems congruent with the strategies that have been selected? If so, the probability of success will be higher than if they are incongruent. For example, a business in an aging industry, experiencing strong competitive pressure on unit cost and productivity, would exhibit higher risk if the managerial system encouraged high creativity and informal reporting, compared to a system demanding tight control, close communications, and rewards for operating efficiency.

Financial Results.   Are the financial expectations (as well as the other measures of performance) easily attainable, or will exceptional performance and luck be required? Irrational expectations on the part of management sometimes produce irrational behavior on the part of the organization.

These sources of risk must be considered in light of other overall questions: Does the business have a history of success? Do the present managers have experience in carrying out the specific strategy selected? Risk is hard to quantify, and managers need to apply judgment to each of the elements in order to derive an overall risk assessment. The decision to proceed or not will then be a question of the risk tolerance of the corporation.

The assessment of corporate performance inevitably entails some measure of risk or predictability. From the investor's point of view, lack of predictability requires a higher return on invested capital, and the stock of the firm will therefore be accorded a higher β.

The total risk experienced by a firm is typically divided into two components: financial risk and business risk. Financial risk represents the uncertainty experienced by the stockholder as the result of financial policy, in particular the adoption of a capital structure that reduces the potential cash flow available to increase the shareholders' value. Thus, a high degree of leverage in the form of long-term debt, for example, might demand that all the firm's free cash be allocated to the bondholders, leaving nothing for the shareholders.

Business risk is the uncertainty experienced by the business itself, separate from the uncertainty arising from capital structure burdens. From a corporate point of view (the vantage point of the manager), the cost of capital could be reduced if cash flow variability could be reduced. But demanding that business managers make better forecasts has not improved the precision of their forecasts. If anything, the reliability of forecasts has exhibited an inverse relation to the amount of energy and money dedicated to improving them. A far more satisfying approach to dealing with the future is to get ready for the unexpected, so as to reduce the trauma of unexpected future events. The prudent manager has a contingency plan to minimize perturbations in future performance without sacrificing the opportunity for future reward.

A standard method corporations used for dealing with future uncertainty in the 1970s was to require managers to develop plans for different contingencies. But managers in most corporations can barely produce one good plan; the quality of most contingency plans barely meets minimum standards. More to the point, however, is that the contingency anticipated is not often the one that materializes, and so the contingency planning exercise becomes irrelevant.

A useful technique for addressing uncertainties in the external environment, however, is vulnerability analysis.[7] The central objective of vulnerability analysis is to identify the underpinnings of a business and hence the threats to these underpinnings. By focusing on those future events having both a high probability of occurrence and a potentially harmful impact on the business, an organization can formulate a limited number of possible responses to the most catastrophic and most probable events. Examples of underpinnings may include resources, stability of costs relative to competitors, technologies, availability of complementary products, and social values. Although this method is applied most frequently at the corporate level, it has equal merit at the level of the business. Figure 8–6 illustrates the format for a typical vulnerability analysis.

Figure 8–6.   Vulnerability Analysis..

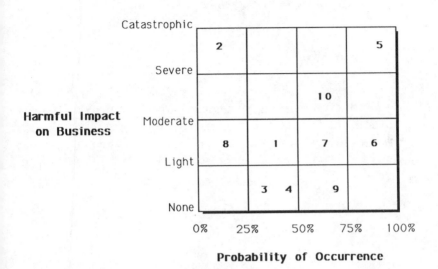

Probability of Occurrence

Note: This is a threat assessment showing composite evaluations and distribution of 10 threats.

Political uncertainty represents a source of risk that has increased in importance, as foreign markets open and the basis of competition shifts from a national perspective to an international or global perspective. In many industries, cost competitiveness has become dependent on the location of offshore production facilities or out-sourcing (in textiles, for example). Increasingly, however, the most competitive locations are found in the most politically unstable countries, as witness developments in South Africa, South America, and most recently, Korea.

Exchange rate risk and the additional issues raised by currency controls and transfer pricing can substantially affect investment valuation, performance criteria, and administrative complexity. While futures contracts and other hedging vehicles provide some insulation against short-term currency fluctuations, adverse long-term movements (devaluation) may impair project payback and the competitiveness of the parent organization.

In evaluating foreign investment, a risk index is sometimes helpful in assessing the relative merits and potential consequences of investment decisions. The components of such an index usually include measures of political stability, economic growth, currency convertibility, productivity, and inflation rate. But only with an environmental scanning system can managers be made aware of changing global conditions.

SUMMARY

The performance of a business or a corporation must be gauged in terms of both economic and strategic criteria, from the viewpoint of its many stakeholders, taking into consideration their relative tolerance for risk. Good performance is the inevitable consequence of implementing sound strategies. Superior performance is the subject of the final chapter.

NOTES

1. In industries having few assets (for example, magazine publishing, where most revenue is derived from advertising), return on sales may be a more useful measure of performance.
2. The FASB (Financial Accounting Standards Board) currently advocates the reporting of cash flow in three categories: operating cash flow (which includes changes in working capital), investing cash flow (including expenditures made for long-term productive assets), and financing (including debt, equity, and dividends).
3. Gordon Donaldson, "Financial Goals and Strategic Consequences," *Harvard Business Review* (May–June 1985).
4. If fixed assets are small, as in the computer software industry, market price correlates more strongly with revenues.
5. Bernard C. Reimann, "Strategy Valuation in Portfolio Planning," *Planning Review* (January–February 1986).
6. Callard, Madden and Associates, "Linking Corporate Performance to Shareholder Value," Chicago, 1985.
7. Douglas A. Hurd, "Vulnerability Analysis in Business Planning," SRI International, Menlo Park, CA, 1977.

9 ACHIEVING SUPERIOR PERFORMANCE

Managers choose to define superior performance in a variety of ways: achieving a set of difficult goals, satisfying all the important stakeholders, surpassing competitors or peers, or eliminating organizational deficiencies. However defined, superior performance is like the holy grail, and, like Sir Galahad, managers have sought it for years, only to see it elude their grasp just as it appears within reach. The management literature has not been helpful. Most published models for excellence prescribe a set of virtues to be acquired; they focus on *what to be* rather than *what to do.*

The recent Peters and Waterman list of managerial homilies, for example, includes "a bias for action," "staying close to the customer," and "sticking to the knitting."[1] Unfortunately, although their book of miracles has found a ready market among managers on the lookout for simple nostrums, the reliability of the findings is questionable. The sample of "excellent" companies is small—and no evidence is presented to show that unsuccessful companies don't have the same qualities. Even more damning is the evidence that by 1984 at least 14 of the 43 firms characterized as excellent in 1978 had fallen from grace, struggling to retain or regain their competitive position.[2] Many failed either to react to economic trends or to adapt to changes in their markets.

Furthermore, a recent analysis of the "excellent" computer companies (IBM, Hewlett-Packard, DEC, NCR, Wang, Data Card, and Amdahl) showed no significant difference from a sister set (Burroughs, Control Data, Sperry, Prime Computer, Cray, and Commodore) in four important dimensions:[3]

- Profitability (including ROS, ROI, and ROE)
- Ratio of market to book value (either absolute or relative to the industry)
- Z (a parameter used to predict bankruptcy)
- Reputation (ability to satisfy stakeholders)

An earlier study provides a plausible explanation of superior economic performance. William Fruhan's research showed that only 72 firms in his sample of almost 1,500 U.S. nonfinancial companies had maintained a return on equity (ROE) greater than 15 percent for 10 successive years (1966–1975).[4] The salient characteristics of the superior performers were the following:

1. Entry barriers to competition
2. Focused product lines
3. High market share
4. Redundant cash
5. Favorable valuation (high market to book value)

Entry barriers (the result of unique products, scale economies, cost advantages, or capital requirements), focused product lines and high market shares produced financial returns greater than the firms' cost of equity capital. These high returns led to excess cash, favorable valuations, and substantial wealth for the shareholders. Even the Fruhan analysis, however, only identifies the attributes of a high economic performer; it does not provide practical guidelines on how to become one.

Borrowing from Eastern traditions, William Torbert suggested the attributes of leaders (or leading firms) to be embodied in the notion of *executive mind,* which he describes as an integration of *observing mind, theorizing mind,* and *passionate mind.*[5] The observing mind develops a clear awareness of the current situation and its dynamics. The theorizing mind identifies significant information, while the passionate mind provides the internal motivation to perform. Torbert recommends the formation of managerial quality circles as an adjunct to a self-study process that can lead to the achievement of the executive mind.

Peter Vaill concluded that high performing organizational systems have clear objectives and strong leaders.[6] These systems have attained a sense of separateness from their environments, and they invest substantial effort in maintaining this sense of separateness. Their leaders commit significant amounts of time to further their objectives, have strong feelings about achieving the system's purposes, and focus on key issues and variables.

Executives such as Konosuke Matsushita, founder of one of the world's largest electronics firms, and Kazuo Inamori, chairman of Kyocera, attribute excellence to the *sunao spirit,* an untrapped mind that is free to identify and exploit opportunities.[7] A *sunao* manager is able to grasp what to do and what to refrain from doing in management. He has the courage to act with clarity of vision and the conviction that his actions are in accordance with the laws of nature.

The models propounded by Torbert, Vaill, and Matsushita may be inspirational. And indeed, they provide us with further insight into the attributes of effective organizations. But they too fail to close the gap left by Peters and Waterman; they fail to give us clear guidance on how to behave or how to manage. This is the mission of the practical strategist.

THE FOURFOLD WAY

Good performance requires selecting an appropriate strategy and implementing it well. The practical strategist extends this model to the limit in order to achieve superior performance. Stated more explicitly, practical strategists realize exceptional results by following these principles (the Fourfold Way, Figure 9–1):

1. They *think strategically*, developing clear plans based on a dominant theme.
2. They *decide to act*, marshalling enthusiastic support for their plans from the entire organization.
3. They *attend to implementation*, applying the necessary functional skills and the appropriate managerial systems.
4. They *adapt quickly* to the changes in their industries, markets, and competitive environment.

Now in a way, this is but a recapitulation of the principles of good management (plan, implement, control). But excellence requires more than a mechanical observance of these principles. Let's examine in more depth each of the major elements of this tetralogy.

Figure 9–1. The Fourfold Way.

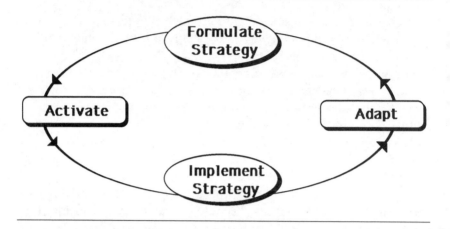

Strategic Thought

Strategic thinking entails a clear logic for the business or the corporation, as we have discussed in previous chapters. The characteristics
that distinguish strategic thinking from the more common operational
thinking include differences in both perspective and focus. Strategic
thinking is concerned with positioning the organization for economic
and managerial renewal. In addition, strategic thinking recognizes the
ultimate objective of strategy to maximize stakeholders' value. Attributes
intrinsic to this perspective include:

A Systems Viewpoint.   Strategic thinking recognizes the critical linkages among the functional activities within the business, and the importance of adding value in the chain from sourcing through customer
sales and service. Operational thinking tends to focus on the effectiveness of each function, independent of the other functions.

Time Perspective.   Strategic thinking recognizes the evolutionary nature
of industries and markets. This recognition is critical to learning from
past experience, responding to current challenges and developing strategies that anticipate future challenges and alternative scenarios. The
preoccupation of operational thinking with current conditions favors
short-term responses and immediate results.

External Orientation.   Strategic thinking recognizes that survival depends more often upon adequately responding to changes in industries

and markets (forces outside the firm) rather than the ability to maximize internal effectiveness and efficiency. The quality of information systems related to the environment, for example, usually takes precedence over internal productivity measurements (although these are also important).

Focus and Dominant Theme.   Strategic thinkers focus on the key success factors within their industries. They target resources at these factors, or at particular markets that are expected to yield desired results. Resource allocation in operationally minded organizations, on the other hand, is frequently dispersed, reflecting an attempt to excel at everything and serve all the markets. This commonly results in serving no markets particularly well or the development of a number of unrelated businesses within the corporate portfolio.

Strategic thinkers challenge the status quo. They ask:

- What are the competitors' strategies?
- What can I learn from customers and suppliers?
- What are my firm's strategic assets, its distinctive competence— and how can I nurture it?
- Where in the value chain should we concentrate our effort?
- What alternatives do we have (break the rules, redefine the industry, establish new alliances)?
- How can we differentiate our firm from competitors and change the competitive equilibrium?
- What are the potential sources of vulnerability and discontinuity?
- Will my strategy work?

No organization achieves distinction in the absence of a clear strategy, but a dominant theme (discussed in Chapter 5) can impel it to greatness and add meaning to its existence—it can be the keystone in the arch of strategy. A dominant theme often derives from a dedication to a particular distinctive competence (such as a technology or functional skill), and customer group. Such a theme is easy to perceive in a new venture established with the clear objective of providing a unique product or service to a specific market segment. As a firm attempts to sustain growth by diversification into new product-market segments, however, the focus may blur, and managers may be unable to assign the right priorities to customers and competitors—witness the erratic results of many conglomerates, such as Litton, Teledyne, and ITT. Diffusion of purpose need not be the inevitable consequence of growth, however.

Du Pont tenaciously retained its technological focus ("Better things for better living through chemistry") until the early 1980s, while 3M's apparent diversity belies its underlying network of linked technology.

These examples should not obscure another crucial role of the dominant theme: to serve as an expression of values, identity, and the organization's dharma or ideal path. When these values permeate the entire organization, strategy acquires meaning, and the members of the organization can commit themselves with enthusiasm and passion to it. Thus, thinking strategically and finding a dominant theme is only the first step. The strategy must be activated.

Activation

Strategy is often disconnected from implementation. To close the circuit requires that the strategist himself be committed. Strategists often experience faintheartedness or weak will. They conceive brilliant strategies, yet lack the energy, resolution, or courage to move forward.[8]

Leadership is central to the activation of the firm and may be the unifying force in attaining superior performance. Leaders often catalyze a strategic vision by telling wonderful stories about the future. They can enunciate the dominant theme and mobilize the energy of the organization behind it. By acting as role models in their behavior, they help define the culture and values of the organization. They bring an attitude that empowers the enterprise to move forward, to adapt, and to take risks.[9]

But even a strong signal from an enthusiastic leader will not suffice if the rest of the organization does not understand it and embrace it with fervor. Achieving commitment, resonance, and the institutionalization of strategy is a particular challenge in organizations undergoing regeneration. Few organizations are blessed with leaders who can provide the vision and transformational energy necessary to adapt to new challenges.[10]

In other words an elegant strategic vision and clearly stated dominant theme will have no force unless the members of the organization align with the vision—unless they share a commitment to implementation. The CEO can march off in any direction he pleases, of course. But a brilliant visionary is likely to fail in an organization if he is unable to marshal the support of his followers. Good leaders get people to follow; they reconcile the need of individuals for autonomy with their need to integrate and become part of a larger whole.

Making the strategy of the firm explicit helps develop commitment, and allowing the key members of the organization to participate in developing the strategic vision can strengthen this commitment. Commitment can subsequently be reinforced in a variety of ways, including the use of appropriate rituals. The Japanese are well known for their use of corporate songs and group exercise to build unity (although the effectiveness of this technique is waning). More important in U.S. organizations is the introduction of systems that reward the successful implementation of strategy.

This raises the issue of appropriate goal setting for the organization. Goals that do not challenge the ability of the organization produce boredom. Excessively ambitious goals, on the other hand, produce anxiety, fear, or paralysis; they sap the morale and vitality of the organization.[11] But aspirations must be set above the limits that may have been accepted previously. John Kennedy, for example, was able to assert that the United States would place a man on the moon before the end of the decade, a goal that was achieved ahead of schedule in July 1969, despite the need to coordinate the contributions of over 400 subcontractors. Most limits are psychological—in allowing no limits, there are no limits.

Implementation

Those who have vision but no ability to realize their vision are dreamers, and their strategies can never be more than dreams unless they are implemented. By the same token, those who have highly developed implementation skills but lack vision are mere mechanics. Organizations that excel in implementing strategy have developed or acquired the right set of functional competencies, backed up by a good managerial system. Implementation, in other words, requires managers and staff who are good at their trade, be it manufacturing, finance, marketing, or some other skill—who have mastered technique. Needless to say, these skills must be relevant to the task at hand, or they have no value. Translated into operational terms, the organization must be competent at carrying out programs that support its strategy.

World champion Edwin Moses won 122 consecutive races in the 400-meter hurdles over a 10-year period. But on June 4, 1987 he lost. After the race, Moses noted that "Instead of thinking about my races technically, I started thinking that if I won I would be successful. And that's dangerous." He observed that "I think losing that race will force me now to pay more attention to running fast rather than running to win. If you run to win, you accept an inferior performance."[12] In other words a strategy of running fast (functional competence) gives the best results. Moses and other superior performers have grasped the importance of mastery.[13]

A corollary to skill in implementation is the need for hard work. Chairman Kim of Daewoo identifies this as an essential differentiator between the success of South Korean firms and U.S. firms. President Kume of Honda observes: "I perspire 99.9% of the time."[14]

Performance will also suffer unless managers install congruent managerial systems—systems that support strategy implementation. After all, managerial systems, including organization, information systems, measures of performance, reward systems, and the other elements previously discussed, constitute the infrastructure of the firm. Implementation falters when the infrastructure gets in the way. It goes without saying, perhaps, that the characteristics of an organization's managerial systems influence strategy formulation as well as strategy implementation, as we have noted previously.

Fervent implementation of an old strategy may not suffice, as Henry Ford and others have found. The practical strategist is attuned as well to the need to adapt, the last element in our model.

Adaptability

Our contemporary organizations have embraced numerous myths. One of the most cherished is the *myth of stability.* Business as usual is a comforting notion, and organizations everywhere enjoy the feeling of safety that emerges when change is slow. Managers and planners, therefore, often direct themselves to the task of preserving the existing stable system and maintaining the status quo. Corporations everywhere have exhibited a pernicious determination to persist in old strategies when the world has changed. The alternatives—deliberately modifying the system or allowing it to evolve—are not often contemplated.[15]

Implicit in this world view is another myth—the *myth of control.* Many managers have the hubris to believe that they can control the environment, or at least those aspects of it that affect their business. The leaders of organizations devoted to stability commit maximum effort to improving forecasts in the belief that the firm can erect appropriate defenses and marshal enough resources to cope with whatever comes. But alas, planners repeatedly forecast the wrong discontinuities, and the future continues to resist definition; stability is a false idol.[16] Recent theories of chaos offer support for this view. Like many other nonlinear disorderly systems, businesses often experience large changes when initial conditions change slightly.

Thus, even though a dominant theme can be timeless, the details of a strategy can rarely endure for more than a few years. Although especially true in embryonic industries, this is also the case in any organization being buffeted severely by change. Firms that cling to old missions (the railroads[17]), to old values (autocratic management), or to obsolete paradigms (national competition) are vulnerable to extinction. A superior organization requires the ability to sense change (or cause change) and adapt to it.[18] Things are fixed before they break.

Stable systems are fail-safe; they minimize the probability of failure by introducing high negative feedback. But these policies often inhibit risk-taking and entrepreneurship. Resilient systems by contrast are safe-fail; they minimize the consequences of failure. More important, the resilient system is consonant with evolution, ultimately the only certain strategy for survival. Thus railroads could become transportation companies, autocratic organizations would anticipate the need to become more participative, and parochial firms could enter global markets.

High-performing organizations transform themselves to meet future challenges. They achieve this adaptability by investing resources in activities that increase their future options. The most obvious vehicle for such investment is R&D, which multiplies the number of future product or process options and leads to economic renewal. But investments in management training and development are at least as important. These investments produce managerial renewal, particularly if they create the attitudes that foster innovation and thinking about the future and enable the organization to learn.[19]

The organization of the future must accept change and adaptation as an intrinsic value. Change in structure, mission, products, and markets, even changes in perceptions and values, must all become part of a new corporate long-life insurance policy. Resilience and adaptability must govern, as opposed to the deceptive stability of the status quo, for survival and growth demands that we learn as we go. The Zen Master Suzuki notes that "In the beginner's mind there are many possibilities, but in the expert's there are few." The practical strategist is prepared to entertain the possibility of strategies and outcomes other than those originally planned, to retain a "beginner's mind."

THE CHALLENGE OF THE 1990s

The next decade will challenge every manager in every organization to become more effective and more efficient, to achieve economic and managerial renewal. This will require managers who understand and apply the principles of practical strategy. To summarize these principles:

- Enunciate a clear strategy and dominant theme. Make purpose and values clear.
- Activate the organization by making a conscious and deliberate personal commitment. Allocate resources explicitly to the strategy. Develop total organizational commitment to realizing the strategy of the organization.
- Install the right functional skills to assure that strategy can be implemented successfully. Establish managerial systems that support the implementation of strategy at every level. Satisfy the need for multiple and complete connections to all the stakeholders inside and outside the organization.
- Adapt quickly to the demands of our dynamic environment, and respond quickly to opportunities and problems. Abandon yesterday's strategy or paradigm if a better one is revealed today. Look for the patterns that suggest new and more inspired responses to challenge.

The next decade calls for a different kind of manager, not the historic navigator or caretaker, but rather an argonaut or bold innovator who can manage by strategy and give balanced attention to implementation. Superior performance, in other words, will arise from acting like a practical strategist, be it at the level of the corporation, the business, or the functional unit.

It is not enough to have a vision. Nor is it enough to be a ruthless enforcer. Within every truly effective enterprise—large or small, new or old, product- or service-oriented—we will find a practical strategist.

NOTES

1. Thomas J. Peters and Robert H. Waterman, Jr., *In Search of Excellence* (New York: Harper & Row, 1983).

2. "Who's Excellent Now?" *Business Week,* November 4, 1984, p. 76.

3. B.S. Chakravarthy, "Measuring Strategic Performance," *Strategic Management Journal,* 7, No. 5 (September–October 1986).

4. William E. Fruhan, Jr., *Financial Strategy* (Homewood, Ill.: Richard D. Irwin, 1979).

5. Cited in Robert J. Allio, "The Executive Mind," *Planning Review* (September–October 1985).

6. Peter B. Vaill, "The Purpose of High-Performing Systems," *Organizational Dynamics* (August 1982).

7. Konosuke Matsushita, *Planning Review* (March 1981).

8. Action without conviction is no better!

9. Not to be confused with Georges Santayana's fanatics, who redouble their efforts when they have forgotten their aim. *(The Life of Reason).*

10. Charles DeGaulle of France during the 1940s, Hyman Rickover of the U.S. Navy's nuclear reactor program during the 1960s, and Margaret Thatcher of the United Kingdom during the 1980s are good role models.

11. Arnold Toynbee correlated economic progress in colonial America with the degree of challenge posed by the environment. In Maine, settlers were totally absorbed with mere survival. In South Carolina and Georgia, living was easy—and industrialization proceeded slowly. In the mid-Atlantic states the challenges were optimal for economic progress.

12. *New York Times,* June 9, 1987.

13. Herbert Simon suggests that 10 years and 50,000 bits of information are required to achieve mastery in "What We Know About the Creative Process," Robert L. Kuhn, ed. *Frontiers in Creative and Innovative Management* (Cambridge, MA: Ballinger, 1985), p. 12. Miyamoto Musashi, the sixteenth-century Japanese samurai, warns that mastery is unlikely to be achieved before the age of 50. (Miyamoto Musashi, *A Book of Five Rings,* [Woodstock, NY: The Overlook Press, 1974], p. 35). Konosuke Matsushita advises that all it takes is practice (Konosuke Matsushita, Editorial, *Planning Review,* March 1982, p. 4).

14. Frederick Hiroshi Katayama, "Japan: Hands on at Honda," *Fortune,* November 9, 1987, p. 88.

15. Although Oswald Spengler understood the world as a "picture of endless formations and transformations of the marvelous waxing and waning of organic forms."

16. Kurt Gödel, the Austrian-born American mathematician and logician, has demonstrated with his incompleteness theorem that uncertainty and undecidability are unavoidable. Werner Heisenberg demonstrates similar intrinsic uncertainty in the physical world with his principle of indeterminacy. And even Chairman Mao observes, "Great disorder in the country leads to greater disorder, and again and again."

17. Could Penn Central have opened an airlines division?

18. A sailing metaphor is remarkably apt. The boat's location corresponds to industry maturity or attractiveness, the quality of the boat and crew corresponds to the resources, other boats represent the competition. A direct course to the finish is unusual, although captains never lose sight of their ultimate destination! More commonly, ships adjust course when the current changes, trim sails when the wind shifts, tack if a direct run is not possible, and alter tactics as a function of the number, skill, and commitment of the competitors, as well as the experience and dedication of their own crews.

19. Even though the future is unknowable, as Henrik Ibsen observes in *Hedda Gabler,* "there are a couple of things to be said about it all the same."

EPILOGUE
PARABLE: A MAN AND HIS STONE

One stormy night, a man came upon a monastery in the forest. He knocked at the thick doors and shouted to be admitted for quite some time, but no one responded. Finally, he found a heavy stone and pounded upon the door. A monk appeared and directed him to a room containing only a sleeping mat. Exhausted, and relieved to be out of the rain, the traveler put his stone on the floor and fell asleep. In the morning when he awakened, he tried to open the door of his room to ask for food, but the door was locked. He shouted, but no one answered. At last, he picked up his stone and pounded on the door. A monk soon appeared and led him into another room, in which were waiting food, water, and a pallet. The traveler bathed, ate, and rested. Once again he sought to leave. Once again he found the door locked, and no one answered his call. When he pounded with the stone, he was again answered and taken to another more comfortable room. And so he went for a number of days, carrying his heavy stone from room to room, and using it to open each succeeding door. Ultimately, he no longer tried the door or shouted, but immediately pounded with his stone when he wanted to leave.

One day, when he was pounding heavily on a door, the monk on the other side said to him, "Why don't you try the door yourself?" The man pushed against the door and it opened easily into the next room. The monk said, "Is it always necessary to carry your heavy stone and beat upon the doors? There are many that are not locked."

Source: From *Planning Review* (November 1980): 47. Reprinted with permission.

INDEX

193

ABOUT THE AUTHOR

Robert J. Allio is recognized internationally as a leading authority in the field of business and corporate strategy. Since founding Robert J. Allio & Associates in 1979, he has spearheaded top-level strategy projects in the United States, Canada, Latin America and Europe; clients include 3M, GTE, Allied-Signal, USX, Dominion Textile, Weyerhaeuser, Banco Popular, and the Canadian Government.

In addition to consulting, Dr. Allio designs and conducts strategy seminars for the Conference Board, *Business Week*, and a broad range of private organizations and professional associations. He was dean of the School of Management at Rensselaer Polytechnic Institute in Troy, New York from 1981 to 1983; he is currently a professor of management at Babson College in Wellesley, Massachusetts, where he teaches policy and strategy.

Prior to 1979, Dr. Allio was a senior consultant with Arthur D. Little in Cambridge, Massachusetts. He has held executive positions with several major corporations, including Canstar, a subsidiary of Noranda Mines (Toronto); Babcock and Wilcox (New York); Westinghouse Electric (Pittsburgh); the United States Atomic Energy Commission (Washington, D.C.); and General Electric (Schenectady).

Dr. Allio created *Planning Review*, the professional strategy journal, in 1972 and served as its editor and publisher until 1985. His previous books are *Corporate Planning: Techniques and Applications* (1979) and *Corporate Planning II* (1986). He has served as president of the North American Society for Corporate Planning and vice president of the International Affiliation of Planning Societies.

When not otherwise occupied, Dr. Allio captains his sloop, Dulcinea, in the New England racing circuit.